The Autobiography of
"One Who Dared to Dream"
MAIDEN NAME: ETHEL MAE MORALE

Heavenly Realms Publishing
Houston, TX

ETHEL MORALE GATHERS

Copyright © 2022 – Ethel Morale Gathers

All rights reserved. This book is protected by the copyright laws of the United States of America. This book may not be copied or reprinted for commercial gain or profit.

Published by: Heavenly Realm Publishing,
www.heavenlyrealmpublishing.com, 1-866-216-0696

Unless otherwise indicated, Scripture quotations are taken from the New American Standard Bible (NASB), Copyright © 1960, 1962, 1963, 1968, 1971, 1972, 1973, 1975, 1977, 1995, by The Lockman Foundation. Used by permission.

ISBN 13—9781944383336 (soft cover)
ISBN 13—9781944383343 (hard cover)

Library of Congress Control Number: 2022908054

1. Autobiography: Autobiography—United States. 2. Autobiography: Autobiography—United States. 3. Autobiography: Autobiography—United States.

This book is available at: Amazon, Barnes & Noble, Books-A-Million, Borders, and stores near you.

This book is printed on acid free paper.

This book is printed in the USA.

The Autobiography of
"One Who Dared to Dream"

MAIDEN NAME: ETHEL MAE MORALE
BORN TO: JOHN MORALE
&
ALIDA (IDA) SENNETT MORALE

TABLE OF CONTENTS

Dedication 6
Acknowledgements 7
Forward 8
Introduction 10
CHAPTER 1 – Origin of Birth... 13
CHAPTER 2 – Ancestry/Family Tree 19
CHAPTER 3 – Birth to Preschool Years.............................. 29
CHAPTER 4 – Elementary School Years............................ 33
CHAPTER 5 – Middle School Years................................... 45
CHAPTER 6 – High School Years....................................... 51
CHAPTER 7 – Military Service 75
CHAPTER 8 – Post Military Service 107
CHAPTER 9 – Federal Civil Service & Retirement 117
CHAPTER 10 – Post Retirement (Present) 129
Notes 143
References 145
Additional Family Pictures 146
Collage 152
About the Ministry 155

DEDICATION

This book is proudly dedicated to my four children by birth, Nathasha, Chastity, LeKeisha and Lauren (Alaina), who, at their request, I write this book.

To my stepsons, Daryl and Michael Gathers, in appreciation of your love and respect throughout the years.

To my thirteen Grandchildren in order of birth: Regis, Felton (Tre), Zharia, Raediance (Rae), Zhyon, Zhyir, Champion (Champ), Zaevion (Zae), Craig Jr (CJ), Z'Carii (Carii), Kingston (King), Zamyr (Myr), and Ayric (Turk).

Lastly, this book is dedicated to my two great-grandchildren, Aaliyah Joi and Saniyah Brielle.

You all are the joy of my life, in whom I thank my God for blessing me to enjoy down to the third generation in the year of our Lord, two thousand twenty-two (2022). My prayer for you is that you live out the words of Jesus, "You shall love the Lord your God with all your heart, and with all your soul, and with all your mind; this is the great and foremost commandment" (Mt. 22:37-38). I also pray for long life according to Psalms 91:16, that I may continue to nurture and to provide guidance for you, enjoying every moment with you! You fulfill my joy!

ACKNOWLEDGEMENTS

To the memories of my late parents, John Morale and Ida Sennett Morale, whose love was unending and who didn't "spare the rod."

To the memory of my late husband of 37 years, Richard Alan Gathers, who always believed in me and always supported my endeavors.

To my remaining siblings, Eva Robertson, Cecelia Peltier, Joyce Robertson, John Morale Jr. (aka Black), and Joseph Morale (aka Ken) for your love and support in all of my accomplishments. Thank you for always being there and knowing that I can always count on you. Thank you for your assistance in writing this book, and for allowing me to rely on your memories where I fell short.

Special thanks to my brother, John (aka Black), my webmaster, my computer engineer, my systems administrator, the family's computer brain! You are such a blessing to our entire family, down to and including the 4th generation. Thank you for your generosity and selfless service to the family. May your hands prosper in all that you do and may God's blessings overflow you.

To all of my Pastors and Teachers, Military and Civilian Leaders who impacted my life, as referenced in this autobiography.

To the Village (Grandparents, Uncles, Aunts, Cousins, Neighbors) who aided in my upbringing, by permission of my parents.

FOREWORD

What A fascinating record of the life of my sister, Ethel Morale Gathers, also known as Lou to her siblings, Mom to her children, Honey to her grandchildren, Elder Gathers to her church associates, and Doctor Ethel Gathers, to those who dare to dream big or "aim high."

I have known Ethel all of her life. Our conversations bring a deep sort of pleasure, always sprinkled with lots of laughter and once in a while a tear or two. Frankly, the older we get, the more I treasure our time together.

Ethel's positive outlook on life, her canny ability to move-on quickly after defeat, and her ability to always be real, or to be herself in any situation, is amazing.

Her #1 attribute, however, is her love and obedience to the Lord, our God. She is steadfast, unmovable, always abounding in the Lord's work, because she knows that her work is not in vain in the Lord (1 Cor 15:58).

This book shares precious moments of Ethel's life (good and bad moments). I have always believed that we create our own surroundings by the thoughts we think. We are sent here to live life fully, to love abundantly, to find joy in our own creations, to experience both success and failure, and to use free will to expand and magnify our lives. Ethel has done this; her autobiography is a testimony!

This book also brings out the wonderful characteristics and teachings of our parents, John and Ida Morale. It uplifts them in their love and wisdom and applauds them for being the wonderful parents they were. I thank God for them.

This record of Ethel's life is a wonderful gift to her children, her grandchildren, her great-grandchildren, and generations to come. It is truly a part of the legacy she leaves for them, as well as for family and friends.

Dr. Joyce M. Robertson

INTRODUCTION

Upon my retirement from civil service on February 29, 2020, I started doing what I had planned to do, TRAVEL. I traveled to Las Vegas with my sister, Joyce, to support my nephew in a play he had written (PATTI) and was starring in. The play was excellent! My brother (Black) met us there and we had a great time. Afterwards, I traveled to Arizona to spend more time with him. It was in AZ we learned that our oldest brother in Kansas City, Mo. (Lloyd/TT) was ill, required immediate surgery, and prognosis was poor. Black said to me, "go and see about our brother." So, I shortened my time with him and traveled to Missouri.

While there, the world entered a pandemic state due to the Coronavirus. I was informed by hospital staff that if I left the hospital for any reason, I would not be permitted to re-enter, as the hospital was going on "lock-down." The hospital graciously permitted me to reside in the private room with my brother. "*Hospitality*" was great. I was permitted to use the shower and toiletries as needed. They provided snacks and occasional meals for me! I stayed three weeks in the hospital room with my brother TT, attending to his needs, until his final day. Reflecting back on a book I read by Dr. Elizabeth Kubler-Ross, "*On Death and Dying*" (Kubler-Ross, 1969), I could recognize the stages as my brother went through the process. Ross describes five stages of death & dying: denial, anger, bargaining, depression, and acceptance (DABDA). I also read small pamphlets *on death and dying* provided by the hospital staff. I found myself identifying the stages, as my brother courageously passed through. I learned a lot by observing him. In fact, I never saw the stage of *anger* in him; he maintained his sense of humor to the end. He never complained about the trials of his life, the hospital course, or his illness. He welcomed prayer and looked to God to bring him through the process. He acknowledged

Jesus Christ as his Lord and Savior; for this I am peaceful and glad! He oftentimes asked me to read to him and to pray for him. I gladly did. At the end of three weeks, he expired peacefully. I'm grateful to God for the three weeks I spent with my brother.

I returned home to San Antonio, TX, broken, overwhelmed and shattered. I was faced with lots of "issues" and was constantly seeking the Lord for guidance. I was somewhat confused about the direction I was to proceed in ministry and needed guidance and clarity from the Lord. On the other hand, while I was grateful to have been allowed to be there with my brother, it was certainly NOT my vision of retirement! I was supposed to be traveling! I already had Brazil in view. I had asked the Lord to allow me to visit every continent on planet earth and He had done just that, with the exception of South America and Antarctica. The latter was not on my bucket list! So, Brazil would be my first adventure upon retirement, so I thought. I also desired to return to the Holy Land, Israel, again. Instead, I found myself quarantined in my own home!

What now? No job, quarantined, church on lockdown, home alone and in despair... That was me. While mopping my floors one day, the Lord inspired me to start writing. I spent countless hours writing, researching, thinking and praying. Whenever one of my children or grandchildren would visit they would ask, "Honey, what are you doing?" I'd simply respond, "writing." When my oldest daughter (Nat) learned that I was writing my first book she said, "Mom when you're done with this one you ought to write a book about yourself." I responded, "I don't need to write about myself, I know all about myself." She replied, "it's not for YOU Mom, it's for the generations after you." She continued, "that would be nice for *us* to have, like the book Aunt Joyce wrote about Grandpa." Five years prior, my sister (Joyce) had published her first book, *"Like Dad Use to Say,"* in memory and honor of our Dad. It was through this book that many of the grandchildren were acquainted with "Grandpa."

Introduction

Within a five-month period I was finishing up my first book: *Church Culture: What Members Dare Not Say*. As I was finishing, my youngest daughter (Alaina) asked, "are you going to write about yourself now?" Later, the same sentiments were echoed by the other two (Chastity and Keisha). Honestly, I had not given any thought to writing an autobiography! But at the request of my children, I thought, what a privilege to be able to leave a legacy in the form of an autobiography, and what an honor that they would ask me to do so.

So, it is at the request of my children that I write this book. I welcome into my life's journey all who read it. May my children, grandchildren, great-grandchildren, and all succeeding generations read and cherish the memories. Welcome to my world.

CHAPTER 1

Origin of Birth

Louisiana
State
State of Louisiana *État de Louisiane (French)*
 **Flag**
 **Seal**
Nickname(s): Bayou State • Creole State • Pelican State (official) Sportsman's Paradise • The Boot

> Motto(s):
>
> Union, Justice, Confidence
>
> Anthem: "Give Me Louisiana"
> "You Are My Sunshine"
> "State March Song"
> "Gifts of the Earth"
>
> **(Excerpt from wickipedia.org/wiki/Louisiana)**

Allow me to briefly introduce you to my home state, Louisiana. For those who may not know, before Louisiana became a state it was first occupied by the Native American Indians, particularly the Opelousa (also Opelousas), the Atakapa, and the Chitimacha tribes. The French "explored" it in the 1660's and established a few trading posts in the following years. A French colonial government soon emerged, with its capital in New Orleans in 1722, four years after the city's founding. Louisiana became an increasingly important *colony* in the early 18th Century.

(The following is an excerpt from wickipedia.org)

The French controlled the Louisiana territory from 1699 until it was ceded to Spain in 1762 under The Treaty of Fontainebleau (Note 1). Spain occupied it from 1762-1801. During the period of French and Spanish rule, many immigrants came to Louisiana from France, the French West Indies (Islands of the Caribbean), Spain, Canada, Germany, Portugal, and some were brought as slaves from Africa. The region became known as the "New France." (wikipedia.org/wiki/New France).

The French and Indian War (1754–1763) pitted the colonies of British America against those of New France (wikipedia.org/wiki/British America). During this war "The Expulsion" occurred. Approximately 11,500 Acadians were deported by the French and Nova Scotia to the Thirteen Colonies. Soon, the Acadians comprised the largest ethnic group in Louisiana. The Louisiana population contributed to the founding of the modern Cajun population (Note 2). The French word "Acadien" evolved to "Cadien," then was anglicized as "Cajun." The ATTAKAPAS chronicles tells of the Acadian's departure from France, and their expulsion from Nova Scotia to their arrival at the Poste des Attakapas, now St. Martinville, Louisiana.

Historically, Louisianians of Acadian descent were also considered to be Louisiana Creoles (Notes 3,4), although Cajun and Creole are often portrayed as separate identities today (Cajuns white/Creoles black). Most Cajuns are of French descent and make up a significant portion of south Louisiana's population and have had an enormous impact on the state's culture.

After the American Revolutionary War (1775-1783), whereby the 13 colonies had gained their independence from Great Britain and became the United States, the U.S. purchased Louisiana from France in 1803 under The Louisiana Purchase, (French: Vente de la Louisiane - Sale of Louisiana). Thus, Louisiana became a State. Counties soon thereafter became Parishes, with the County Seat in Opelousas, La., named after the Opelousa Indians who had fought to maintain their independence (Chidsey, Donald Barr. Louisiana Purchase. Crown Publishers, Inc., New York. 1972.)

In summary, Louisiana was maintained by the French from 1699-1762; partly by the British in 1763; by the Spanish from 1763–1800; re-acquired by the French from 1800–1803; and finally purchased by the United States in 1803 under The Louisiana Purchase. Howbeit, France only controlled a small fraction of this area, with most of it inhabited by Native Americans. For the majority of the area, what the United States bought was the "preemptive" right to obtain Native American lands by treaty or by conquest, to the exclusion of other colonial powers.

Birthplace. Welcome to my birthplace, Arnaudville, La.

Arnaudville sits on the original site of an Attakapas Indian village and is one of the oldest remaining towns in St. Landry Parish. The French settled this area in the 18th Century. First called "La Murière" (French for "the rain"), it was later known as "La Jonction" by its French-speaking citizens since Arnaudville is located at "the junction" of Bayou Teche and Bayou Fuselier. Part of Arnaudville is located in St. Landry Parish while the other part is located in St. Martin Parish (wikipedia.org/wiki/Arnaudville, Louisiana).

In the 19th century, the town was named after the Arnaud Brothers who had donated a large amount of land to the town to make a Church for whites and a Church for blacks (which still exists today). Many of their descendants still live in the area. Arnaudville was incorporated in 1870.

Est. 1870. (Picture and information from Wikipedia.com)

According to the United States Census Bureau, the town has a total area of 0.7 square mile, all land. Population in 2020 was 1398. Racial makeup is 88.63% white, 10.73% African American, .07% Native American, .50% two or more races, and 1.57% Hispanic/Latino. Over age 5, 65.1% are English speaking and 34% are French speaking.

Today, the town is host to the *Étouffée Festival* held the 4th weekend in April, *Le Feu et l'Eau* (Fire and Water) Rural Arts Celebration held in December, and *Bayou Blues Revival* held in April. Boudin sausage, crawfish etouffee, gumbo, spicy shellfish or chicken and rice dish is common at an annual festival. Since 2005, the town has become a haven for artists and musicians from around the world. The Cajun fiddle is associated with Arnaudville. It is not unusual to hear four-string masters sawing away in spontaneous jam sessions. Zydeco musicians host festivals all through the year. Its thriving arts community is centered in the old part of town.

Welcome to my birthplace, Arnaudville, Louisiana 😊.

CHAPTER 2

Ancestry/Family Tree

	PATERNAL	MATERNAL
Great Grandparents	Juan Morales (Canary Islands, Spain) & Marianne Marguerite Masse	UNKNOWN & Onesimus Sennett
Grandparents	Joseph Bartolino Morale & Cecelia Miller Morale	Ignace Sennett & Eva Bergeron-Sennett
Parents	John Morale	Alida (Ida) Sennett-Morale
Self **Children** (born to Ethel & Richard Alan Gathers)	Ethel Mae Morale, born November 15, 1951 Nathasha Lynette Gathers (Jefferson), Chastity Yvette	

Ancestry/Family Tree

Grandchildren	Gathers, LeKeisha Ellen Gathers, Lauren Alaina Gathers **Children of Nathasha:** • Regis Isaiah Gathers • Felton Bernard Brady III • Zharia Tiyona Sullivan	
	Children of Chastity: • Champion Kordell Williams • Zavion Boss-Kord'e Williams • Kingston Kori-Mekhi Williams	
	Children of LeKeisha: • Radiance Auriel Howard • Craig Lavan Jr. • Ayric Craig Lavan **Children of Lauren (Alaina):** • Zhyon Sincere Spears	

	- Zhyir Jha'Mal Spears - Z'Carii Lyric-Danielle McGarity - Zamyr Christian McGarity	
Great Grandchildren	**Child of Regis Isaiah Gathers** - Aaliyah Joi Gathers	
	Child of Felton Bernard Brady III (Tre) - Saniyah Brielle Brady	

Ancestry/Family Tree

**Joseph B. Morale and Cecelia Miller Morale
Paternal Grandparents**

John Morale & Ida S. Morale
Parents

Ancestry/Family Tree

Richard A. Gathers & Ethel M. Gathers

**Nathasha, Chastity, LeKeisha, Alaina
Children & Me**

Ancestry/Family Tree

Grandchildren

**Great-grandchildren
Aaliyah and Saniyah**

CHAPTER 3

Birth to Preschool Years

While I cannot attest to anything prior to my pre-school years, I am told that I was born in our family home in Arnaudville, Louisiana, November 15, 1951, and delivered by a mid-wife. Health insurance was uncommon then, particularly for poor Blacks. Therefore, most black babies were delivered in the homes by mid-wives. I was the 12th of 15 children born to John Morale and Ida Sennett. I salute my Mom for birthing without the use of anesthesia, IV, epidural or any modern medicine or procedure available today. My Mom lost three of the 15 children at birth/infancy, so I was the 9th of 12 children raised by my Mom and Dad. Large families were common then; these family sizes are unheard of today!

Mid-wives were not required to be licensed back then. There were no schools or formal training for mid-wives as exists today. Women in this era learned from each other how to deliver and care for babies! They learned from each other the practice of boiling water to sterilize instruments, cutting of the umbilical cord and tying it with a string, and putting a band over the baby's belly-button to keep it from protruding. It was also believed that this practice would strengthen the baby's back. I remember the stories that my Mom would tell, of how they delivered and nursed each other's

Birth to Preschool Years

babies. Many mothers had babies within 10-13 months apart. Therefore, it was not uncommon for mothers to have two babies requiring nursing at the same time, or two babies in diapers at the same time. Therefore, if one mother's milk supply was insufficient to nurse 2 babies, her sister or close relative would nurse one of the babies from her own breast. To that we said "ughhhhh," but communal living was the way of life.

If the family was of the Catholic faith, it was a requirement of the mid-wife to report information of a child's birth to the local Catholic Church. If the mid-wife had a 'busy day,' delivering two or more babies in the same day or in close proximity, information was oftentimes reported late. Illiteracy and lack of transportation could have very well added to this delay. Therefore, information reported was oftentimes incorrect, or the midwife may not have remembered the name of the child given by the parents. The Church would record the birth information and in-turn, report it to the County seat, Opelousas at the time. Original documents were oftentimes lost; legal documents were oftentimes with error.

For example, my 2nd cousin and I were born in the same month and year and delivered by the same midwife. My cousin's first name was Mary Alice. Somehow the information got misconstrued and my name was reported as "Mary Alice Morale," though my parents named me "Ethel Mae Morale." Consequently, my birth name was reported incorrectly to the County seat and documented incorrectly on my birth certificate. Parents were oftentimes left out of the loop and did not receive a copy of the birth certificate. It became their responsibility to order from the County Seat. This posed a significant problem as many were illiterate, including my parents. This was the status of many farmers in the 1940's-1960's; the wherewithal did not exist for them to order legal documents. It wasn't until I joined the military at age 18 that my birth certificate was obtained and subsequently corrected.

The Catholic Church would issue a 'Baptism Certificate' at the time of a baby's baptism. This document carried a lot of weight and was regarded an official legal document. The Baptism Certificate was oftentimes used in place of a birth certificate, particularly for school registration.

Coupled with the problem of information being misconstrued on legal documents, was the practice of the Catholic Priest changing a baby's given name, particularly when it was not a "Biblical" name. The Priest would change the name prior to reporting it to the County seat, sometimes without informing the parents. An example of this was the naming of two of my brothers. They were named Emery Morale (born in 1953) and Kenry Morale (born in 1955) by my parents. However, their names were reported to the county seat as John Morale and Joseph Morale respectively and documented on their birth certificates as such. This practice called for many correction requests to the Bureau of Vital Statistics whenever these discrepancies were discovered. So, my brothers were known throughout their educational years as Emery and Kenry, the names selected by my parents. It wasn't until graduation from High School that our birth certificates were corrected, as we moved toward enlistment into military service or as we pursued other goals.

At approximately age 4, I can recall my oldest sister, Eva, bringing me to visit her school. The school offered "young sister/young brother visitation day" and she would bring me as her guest. I was so happy, not to visit the classroom per-se, but to dress up and to wear my Easter patent-leather shoes! That was a peak in my childhood years! I liked attending church services on Sundays because I got to dress up and get my hair washed and pressed, another highlight! I had long, thick hair, and at a young age I learned to take pride in dressing up and looking pretty 😊.

Birth to Preschool Years

My sister, Eva, was like a second mother to my sister, Joyce, and me in our earlier years of childhood. With Mom's hands being full (having babies every other year), and with Eva being the oldest girl, she was oftentimes called upon to assume motherly roles. For instance, she would prepare bath water for us, wash and comb our hair, leaving a lasting memory! Her frustrations coupled with our thick, coarse hair was not a good combination. She would sit us on the floor and lock her legs across our bodies in order to comb our hair (and to keep us from running off). If we placed our hands on our heads to alleviate the pain, she would pop our hands with the comb or brush. It was a war that we always lost; Eva was determined to win, and she did every time! I can recall Eva preparing our meals, washing and ironing our clothes, and laying it out for us the evening before we needed them.

That's the way it was then, the older siblings helped the younger ones! I am grateful today for the sacrifices she made in helping to raise my sister Joyce and me, and our three younger brothers. I am equally grateful to my three older brothers (Roy, Lloyd and Floyd, now deceased) who sacrificed part of their educational years, not by choice, but because our Dad required assistance in the fields to provide for the family. God blessed our upbringing through it all!

CHAPTER 4

Elementary School Years

Preschool and kindergarten did not exist then (early 1950's) in Arnaudville. A child stayed home with parents until age six then started first grade. Entry into first grade was also permitted at age 5 as long as the child's birthday occurred before December 31st of the school year. So, with a birthday in November, I was permitted to start **1st grade** at the age of 5, at Huron Elementary School in Arnaudville, La.

HURON ELEMENTARY SCHOOL, ARNAUDVILLE, LA.

Elementary School Years

Schools were segregated then, so all Black kids attended Huron Elementary School. Again, I was happy to attend school because it meant that I would get my hair pressed and combed nicely every day! I'd get to wear my new clothing, most of which Mom hand made. Mom was a seamstress who could turn old garments into new at a heartbeat. She used no patterns; she just 'knew' our fit. I was excited about learning to read and write also. I found education fascinating. I learned the difference in grades (A, B, C, D, F) at an early age. I learned that A was the best and F was the worst. Occasionally, the teacher would grant an A+ to distinguish great work! I liked A+ and I wanted to be an "A" student. I didn't even know what a goal was then but looking back I see now that wanting to be an A-student WAS a goal! I wanted to make A's because that was the best; Mom and Dad had instilled in us, "do your best." I enjoyed reading then and still do today. I enjoyed being able to understand a story written in words, an opportunity that unfortunately neither of my parents had.

Sunday afternoon was normally visitation time. An 'outing' was to first attend church service at our local Catholic Church, come home and eat Sunday dinner, then go out and visit our relatives, or they would visit us. Our parents understood and taught us the value of family and having "manners." We were not allowed to address any adult by their first name. Every adult had a prefix to their name, i.e., Aunt, Uncle, Cousin, Ma 'dame (Madam/Miss), or Monsieur (Mister/Sir). Questions were answered with "Yes Ma'am," "Yes Sir," "No Ma'am," or "No Sir." That was how we honored and respected the older generations and people in authority. This teaching carried on into all settings – Church, home, relatives & friend's homes, and the entire community.

Our community was French speaking. Rather, the 'creole dialect' was dominant. Everyone in the community spoke or at least understood the creole language. Most parents spoke the Creole language to their children in the homes. Even when we visited relatives and friends, the Creole language was spoken. Therefore, when we started school, we were more proficient in the Creole language than in the English language! I can remember the teachers telling us (in an effort to help us learn the English language), "No speaking Creole in the classroom!" So, we were forced to learn the English language fluently. We oftentimes mixed the two languages, particularly when we didn't know an English word, we would substitute a Creole word. One would think this would pose an embarrassment, but it did not, as 90% of the students were in the same boat! Children looked forward to going outside for recess, we couldn't wait to speak the Creole language. We were more comfortable with the Creole language than with English. However, when we returned to the classroom, it was English all over again. I enjoyed going to school, being with my friends and cousins, and making good grades.

As children, we were not given a choice as to whether we were going to church or not. It was understood that we were going. It was a must; it was the norm. At approximately age seven, **2nd grade**, I was attending Saturday school, Catechism as it was called. As Catholics, we learned the basic tenets of the Roman Catholic faith. We learned about the sacraments and about going to confession. By age seven also, I made my First Communion and began taking Holy communion. Whatever principles and sacraments we learned, we practiced as well. Occasionally our family would not have transportation to go to church. However, that was no excuse for not attending church service according to Dad and Mom. We would WALK at least 7 miles to attend church service on Sunday. Oftentimes if someone had a large enough vehicle they would stop and offer us a ride. Sometimes there was not enough room for the entire family, so my Dad would allow my Mom and the younger ones to ride; everyone else had to keep walking! Occasionally a farmer on a tractor with a hitched wagon would stop and offer us a ride. There was no room for *pride* and *embarrassment* in those days, we'd gladly jump into the wagon to avoid the long walk! I remember one Sunday the Priest used our family as an example of *"determination"* and *"dedication."* He told the congregation how "the Morale family is here on time even if they have to walk!" My Parents were ever so proud that day, just to be called out in a positive light in front of the entire Congregation.

As a **3rd and 4th grader**, eight and nine years old, I was still excelling greatly in school, making the Honor Roll every grading period at Huron Elementary. Although the schools were segregated (all Black population), it's sad to admit that we became acquainted with "prejudice" even within our own race at such an early age. It appeared that lighter-complexioned Blacks were favored by "some" teachers. Today we call it *"colorism,"* the practice of showing preference to those of a lighter skin color within groups of people of the same race. Also, children whose parents did volunteer work at the school or church seemed to "get by." Students who had "good" or "long" hair were favored by a few teachers. We referred to them as "teacher's pets." Well, my siblings and I didn't fit into any of the "favored" categories. However, there were a few teachers who valued hard work and good behavior. They favored my siblings and me; I guess we were "their" pets!

My Dad was a Farmer, the best in the region. He was favored by the white landowners because he brought them "much gain." Dad understood the proper seasons for planting, and the proper crop for the season. He planted cotton, sweet potatoes, Irish potatoes, okra, and corn, the main crop. Occasionally he'd try something new, like squash and snap beans. He was a hard worker who took pride in his work. He always wanted to be FIRST in everything. First to plant, first to harvest, first to finish his crop. He had to produce the *best* crop and the *most* crop. He worked as a sharecropper, meaning he lived on the land (rent-free) and farmed the landowner's land. Landowners and sharecroppers would enter an agreement as to the percentage a sharecropper would receive and the percentage the landowner would receive on the proceeds from the crop. I believe my Dad earned two-thirds from the sale of the produce while the white landowner received one-third. I attribute my hard work ethics in school to my Dad's work ethics on the farm.

Farm work was hard. We would attend school during the day. Immediately upon returning home from school, we would change into our "field clothes" and proceed to the fields until sundown. Mom was a home maker. She maintained the home and ensured we had hot meals before and after school and when we returned home from the fields. As children we had chores. Girls fed the chickens, roosters and ducks; boys fed the pigs, horses, mules and cows. Boys also milked the cows, while girls helped Mom with laundry, dishes, cooking, and mopping floors. Today, my Dad would be considered a male chauvinist ☺. Our water and bathrooms (out-houses) were located outdoors. So, for baths we drew water from the outside pump (or well), heated it up in buckets, then poured it into a larger tub in order to take a bath. Our drinking water was also pumped into buckets and brought indoors. In-between dinner and baths, we did our homework and studied for tests.

If it sounds like life was tough, fortunately we didn't know it! That was the normal lifestyle for most Blacks (and few Whites) in the region! Thankfully, we never missed a meal; farm life offered the best of meals! Mom's garden afforded us fruits, mostly watermelon, cantaloupe, and tomatoes. Dad's fields and livestock afforded us the vegetables and meats. I dare not leave out Dad's hobbies of fishing and hunting! His "catch" also contributed to food on the table: fish, turtle, eel, rabbit, alligator and crocodile were among his "catch." Occasionally he would go "crabbing" and take us with him. He taught us how to catch crabs by tying the bait in the center of a net and lowering the net into the waters. He taught us how to "crawfish" by putting bait at the end of a string and lowering it into the waters. Yes, good old country living! I may as well add that Dad was skilled at trapping possums, racoons, and armadillos; whatever he caught, Mom cooked, and we ate!

I was sitting in my **5th grade** classroom one day and Dad came to the school to pick us up early. Only my two younger brothers and I were still at Huron Elementary school. My sisters were in Jr. High and High School. It was mid-day, very unusual because Dad never picked us up from school unless it was raining; we walked to and from school. Little did we know, he had accepted another job as a sharecropper in another city/Parish. The principal came to get us from our classrooms. We saw Dad sitting in the office and didn't understand what was going on. That's when he told us we were moving. "Moving where?" We asked.

"Carencro" he said.

Carencro? Where on earth is Carencro? We didn't know. The principal, Mr. Thomas, walked with us and Dad to the car and talked with my Dad along the way. The consolation I remember as a 5th grader was when the principal asked my Dad, "Why are you doing this to me?"

"Doing What?" My Dad asked.

"You're taking away my BEST students."

Dad simply laughed and said, "you'll get some more."

His *BEST* students? We certainly didn't know it! I hardly remember being a "teacher's pet," (ok, maybe "favored" by one). We never had preferential treatment! I do remember being "friended" by the teacher's pets and feeling "accepted" by the group; Meanwhile, they were copying my homework assignments! But it felt good to be included with the "popular girls" - the teacher's pets! In retrospect, I do recall two years prior that the same principal had moved my younger brother (Black) from 2nd grade to 3rd grade in the middle of the school year. He felt that my brother was able to work at a higher grade level. I don't think he ever discussed this with my parents. That's how it was done then! It was enough consolation to me to be called *"best students"* by the principal.

Move to Carencro, Louisiana

I felt bad about leaving my first cousin and best friend behind (Louella Morale, aka "Black") who was also my classmate. Black and I had started first grade together and we were like sisters. My Mom would occasionally allow me to spend the night at her house. Her Dad and my Dad were brothers. Thank God for family values! After our move, my parents still took us back to Arnaudville to visit our relatives, so I was able to see her. On the other hand, I was so glad that I wouldn't have a certain teacher the following school year! Many of the kids said she was MEAN, and she whipped children a lot! Hard and abusive was she! Spanking was legal in the schools then, and she took advantage of it! Today she would be charged with child(ren) abuse and fired!

Schools and churches were also segregated in Carencro. So, we were enrolled in Carencro "Negro" Elementary School, named as such to distinguish it from the all-White Carencro Elementary School. Blacks attended the all-black school; Whites attended the all-White school. With the uprising of racial tension and discrimination in the early 60's, the name of the school was later changed to "Carencro Heights Elementary School."

Elementary School Years

CARENCRO HEIGHTS ELEMENTARY SCHOOL, CARENCRO, LA.

Carencro is located in the suburbs, 7 miles outside the city of Lafayette, La. We lived in the farmland part of the city, then known as "Prairie Boss." The kids at school would tease us and call us "the girls from the Prairie." It was different. A few of the kids understood a few creole phrases (from their parents). None of the kids spoke the creole language fluently. But it was ok, as we were now fluent in English. However, after school, it was back to creole language at our home.

Life on the farm in Carencro was similar to that of Arnaudville. Houses were about 1-3 miles apart. Water was still brought in from an outdoor pump, and the bathroom (toilet) was still outdoors. A big difference, however, was the spacious house and spacious land upon which we lived! The house was located on approximately 4 acres of land. On Saturday afternoons Dad would let us out of the fields a little early. He would set up "bases" in the pastureland and we would play games such as baseball, badminton, dodgeball, and similar games. Occasionally he would saddle up the horses and allow us to enjoy horseback rides. Of course, music and dancing were always included; Dad was a jokester and a dancer! On rainy days, Mom would take charge of the games which predominantly consisted of bingo and card games. Yes, growing up on the farm was hard work, but great work ethics were instilled in us by our parents, and it has paid off; they are engrained in us today!

In Arnaudville, we walked to school; in Carencro, we were pretty excited about riding the school bus! The distance from our house to the street was approximately one-fourth of a mile. On rainy days we would wait until the school bus would pass our house and make a U-turn at the end of the road; we would meet it upon return. Our neighbors' kids would come to our house to catch the school bus with us. They became our friends and a few of us were in the same class. Their parents were farmers also, so the kids were acquainted with field work. It was good to make friends so quickly.

For the first time in my life, I experienced what a "teacher's pet" really felt like, so did my siblings. However, this was a different favoritism! The teachers in Carencro seem to favor and appreciate hard-working students, students who took pride in their work. I must admit, it felt great to be accepted and favored! At Carencro Elementary School, an "Honor Roll List" was posted in the main hallway of the school. So, everyone knew who the "Honor Roll Students" were. Every grading period, all four of us (my sister Joyce, myself, Emery and Kenry) would make the list. So, we quickly became known as a "smart family." It helped that we had 2 sisters in High School (Ella and Mercedes). If we needed assistance, they were honor students as well!

Again, I accredit my parents for instilling good work ethics in us, although Dad was the great motivator! *"Ci zous pas-pa, za romoces koton"* (If ya'll don't pass, ya'll gonna' pick cotton). Well, what better motivation did we need? It was enough that after school we worked in the fields until sundown! We certainly didn't want to do this all day! So, we studied hard and did our best in school, understanding at an early age that graduation from high school was our ticket off the farm!

At Carencro Elementary School we gained new friends and new teachers. There were no such thing as exchanging classes. We had what was known as a "Home-room teacher," and all classes were taught by the same teacher, including physical education. School was fun, we made the best of the move.

Meanwhile, Dad and Mom kept us in touch with our relatives back in Arnaudville. A fun night was when I got to spend the night at my uncle's house with my first cousin, my best friend, Louella (Black). One night my aunt placed blackberries on the table, she intended on making blackberry pies. Meanwhile, Black and I were "helping ourselves" to the blackberries, dropping a few on the floor here and there while sneaking them to Black's room. Well, my aunt discovered the blackberries were tampered with. She also knew who the culprits were (those with a blue mouth and blackberry stains on their clothing), Black and me. Our punishment was to get on our knees and stay there until we repented and asked for forgiveness. Very constructive, yet Black and I were very stubborn and would not repent. We concluded that "if we repent, she will whip us anyway," so we agreed to just stay on our knees. After remaining on our knees for about an hour (or two), our kneeling position soon became a lying-down position, which quickly turned into sleep. My aunt left us there, until we awoke and went to bed. The next day I thought, "we got off easy; My Mom would have handled it differently!"

Mom was a "no-nonsense" kind of woman. She said what she meant and meant what she said. In all actuality, she was the disciplinarian among our parents. That's what it was called then, discipline. Spanking was a "legal" form of discipline and Mom exercised her right, though she was just and fair. Mom visited her sister one day, (Aunt Louella, aka Toot-Toot) who lived in the city

(Lafayette). She found my first cousin, Linda, three years old at the time, outside, unaccompanied by an adult. Her parents were not home. Long story short, Mom packed Linda's clothing and brought her home to live with us. Mom was the oldest of 6 girls and Toot-Toot was the youngest. She simply told Toot-Toot "you're not ready to raise a daughter, I'm keeping her here." There was no discussion, no argument. Frankly, I think Toot-Toot was relieved; she had 2 other children. So, Linda lived with us and became a "little sister" to us.

Approximately 5 years following our move to Carencro (1962), with the family decreasing in size, Dad bought his own property and had his own house built. Praise God! Farming as well as our family size was decreasing. My three older siblings, Cecelia, Ella, and Mercedes had graduated from High School and moved on. For the first time we had an indoor bathroom and indoor running water! We had lights we could turn on by flipping a switch as opposed to pulling a string. We felt rich! No more outhouses, no more drawing water from the outside pump and heating it up in order to take a bath. We had a built-in bathtub! What a blessing and how happy and proud we were. We would go to school and tell our friends about our new house!

Mom hosted a card game at our new house. It was on a weekend and our cousins, nieces and nephews were there. This meant playing games such as hide-n-seek, cowboys-&-Indians, shooting marbles, playing jacks, racing games and such, FREE games. While the adults were engaged in their card game, the children decided to pop firecrackers. This was fun, until "somebody" lit a firecracker and threw it inside the wooden storage shed (called a wash house then) located behind our house. Inside the wash house was a washer/dryer unit, and storage items such as a lawn mower, gasoline cans, and garden tools. Well, the firecracker ignited either the clothing or perhaps the gasoline can. Before we knew it, the shed was up in smoke! Needless to say, it busted up the card game and all the surrounding neighbors came running to our house to help put out the fire! It was pretty scarry, as the flames were moving toward the house itself. Thank God they succeeded! We (the children) were scared! No one ever owned-up to shooting the firecracker inside the shed! As adults today, we laugh about it at family gatherings, accusing one another and pointing fingers as to "who" really started the fire.

CHAPTER 5

Middle School Years

In Carencro there was no "Middle School" as we know it today. Elementary School consisted of first through eighth grade. High school consisted of ninth through twelfth grade. Therefore, I completed my elementary years and middle school years at the same school, Carencro Heights Elementary.

Those were happy years for me! I excelled in school, had great teachers who appreciated hard working students. I met new friends. Life was good. Though there were a few fighters and bullies at the school, the faculty handled them pretty well. They either received spankings by the teacher or principal, or in a worst-case scenario they were expelled and sent home. I recall this bully in my 6th grade classroom. I was actually afraid of her, and she knew it! She picked on me at every opportunity. I can recall my sister, Joyce, confronting her; Joyce was in 7th grade and had not experienced being bullied. She confronted the bully one day, and in the hallway of the school while the bully was drinking from the water fountain, Joyce went and pushed her head down upon the fountain and said, "leave my sister alone!" I think Joyce took off running afterwards. Needless to say, the bully never retaliated against Joyce; In fact, she actually lightened up on me! 😊

Middle School Years

While my Dad taught us to "turn the other cheek and walk away," my Mom taught us to take up for one another and "stand your ground." This meant, protect one another, and fight in defense of one another if necessary. I took up for my three younger brothers in school, just as when the bully came after me, my sister Joyce came to my aid. We weren't really fighters. We just had to war-off bullies! I remember a girl throwing a rolled-up paper in my face on the school bus; she was our neighbor. When we got off the bus, I threw a paper (hard) in her face! We started fighting but it didn't last long. The older ones separated us. That was the only fight I had in 12 years of school!

In the **6th grade** I decided to run for "Queen" of our school. Winning was contingent upon raising the most money for the school, sad to say. Well, in the middle of the contest period, Mom decided we couldn't afford it anymore. Other contestants were selling popcorn balls, candid apples, raffle tickets, etc. But they were not farm girls! Their only responsibility was school. I still had work after school and home chores after the field work. My Mom decided I should drop out because we couldn't keep up with the other contestants. I was so crushed and embarrassed. My 6th grade teacher, Ms. Harris, tried to console me. She was nice, but I still felt the embarrassment! But I must admit, after I dropped out of the race, the pressure was off!

On November 22, 1963, our country suffered a great loss, the assassination of our President, John F. Kennedy. I recall teachers and students crying and the school being called to prayer. When we arrived home from school that day, Mom had the TV turned off and Dad was NOT in the fields! Very unusual! Mom was quiet and the house was in "mourning" mode - tv off, candles burning, lights off. Well, as children we didn't quite understand the impact, but to Dad and Mom it was HUGE! They had apparently voted for John F. Kennedy as President and said, "the country killed a good man."

It was sad to see my Parents in sorrow. Dad had been drinking his "Morgan David" wine; he was on his knees praying and crying at the same time. He had a handkerchief in his hand and as we walked through the door he asked, "y'all heard what happened today?" We said "yes, we prayed at school." He was wiping his eyes saying "c'est triste, c'est triste" (it's sad, it's sad). I had only seen my Dad cry once, when my Grandmother (his Mom) passed away. My brothers and I couldn't hold it in! We went in the back room and started laughing at the site! A drunk man, on his knees praying and crying, with a handkerchief in his hand and a bottle of Morgan David wine at his side; I still chuckle at the thought of the sight today. Needless to say, we were glad to be exempt from working in the fields that day!

In the **7th grade** (11-12 y/o), I decided I'd try out for the basketball team. I enjoyed sports, but soon found out the girls on the team were "rough!" Besides, my Dad had a problem with my attending practice immediately after school, so basketball was short-lived. After all, there was always "something" to do in the fields! Cotton to pick, sweet potatoes to dig up and crate, okra to break, squash or snap beans to pick …. always something! My Dad believed certain jobs were for boys only, and certain jobs were for girls only. Therefore, only boys could break corn, so the girls got lucky! That's the only job in the fields which girls were exempt from doing! He'd say *"va idday zouz Mo-Mo dans la maison"* (go and help your Mom in the house). Well, Mom's motto was "A woman's work is never done." So, as clean as the house appeared to us girls, Mom could always find *something* for us girls to do, even if it meant cleaning the yard! I mean, cleaning up what the animals had left behind! Ughhhhh! So, with sports being out the way, I resulted to participating in school plays and school dances, which took place during school hours.

Other than those two incidents with the bully, the run-for-queen dropout, and the basketball team dropout, my middle school years

Middle School Years

were great! I excelled academically throughout my middle school years and gained favor with my teachers. I think I got my first real taste of being a "Teacher's pet" in middle school 😊. My 6th grade teacher (Ms. Harris) and my 8th grade Teacher (Mr. Henderson) favored me. I believe they appreciated my work ethics. I studied hard and was the best student I could be; they appreciated that. My first serious "crush" on a boy in my class happened in the 7th grade. But what was the use? He was too advanced, and I didn't have permission to go anywhere at age 12. I feared my parents, so skipping class was NOT an option. So, the crush died off as he moved on to another girl who apparently had more freedom!

In the **8th grade** at age 13, I was selected to represent my class at a speech competition at a high school in Lafayette, the city. I was scared. I was a bit intimidated by the "city kids." Instead of feeling "honored" that my teacher would pick *me* among 25 students to represent the class, I was afraid and intimidated. So intimidated that I asked one of my friends if she would read the poem, a poem I had written. The teacher got wind of it and called me to her office and gave me a good lesson on "self-esteem." We didn't talk back to teachers then, we just listened. I remember her telling me "You're under-estimating yourself!" She began to convince me that I could do this, and that my poem was the best one written in the class! I went home and told Mom, who gave me a greater lesson on believing in myself. After two consultations, I was convinced that I could do it, and I did. That experience opened my mind to greater possibilities of what I could do. This was just the beginning! Little did I know I was being prepared for high school the following year (with the city kids) and life thereafter!

It was in the 8th grade also, a particular young man in my class took a liking to me! I didn't know what to do with that! I had never had a real "boyfriend" before and didn't know how to respond. In fact, it was 'embarrassing' to me whenever he'd try to talk to me alone. He wasn't embarrassed; he had previously had other girlfriends!

Besides, there was just no time for boyfriends, so I brushed him off and settled for having "secret crushes" on boys! My parents were strict. We were not allowed to have boyfriends at that age. Remember, I started first grade at age five, so my classmates were a year (or two) older than me. They were also "city boys," which my Dad did not trust.

Whenever we went out, we were chaperoned by an adult, either an aunt or uncle, or my Dad himself! So, on weekends we looked forward to attending school dances, church dances, or our favorite spot, Rocket Beach! Rocket Beach was a club, with a man-made hole in the ground away from the club, which they convinced us was a "beach." But that was the "hot spot" then. Rocket Beach was located in Opelousas, La. (named after the Opelousa Indians), approximately 17 miles away. The kids at school would make plans to party there on weekends. Alcohol was not sold at Rocket Beach. Besides, we were not permitted to drink anyway. Rocket Beach was surrounded by lights, resembling Christmas tree lights. It was about a 20-minute ride which seemed to take forever because we were so anxious to get there! As we would approach Rocket Beach we'd start singing "I see the light, I see the light, I see the party lights..." We paid 50 cents to get in. My sister's cheap boyfriends sometimes didn't want to pay the 50 cents, so they would hide in the trunk of the car! There was no shame in their game! Those were the fun days. We danced to the music of LIVE BANDS, real talented musicians, until the club closed! Rocket Beach was the spot for high-school age and young adults! Then we were returned home by the chaperon.

As embarrassing as it was then, today I'm very thankful for my upbringing. I'm thankful for parents who raised us with morals and provided security and protection for us. I'm thankful for the work ethics they instilled in us. Though we couldn't wait to leave the farm life, I look back now and can only appreciate it and thank God for parents who loved us and cared for us. To God be the Glory!

CHAPTER 6

High School Years

Farm life continued as I entered High School. There was no middle school graduation then, you simply moved to the next grade, or you repeated that same grade if you didn't meet the qualifications to "pass." There was no "repeating" in my family; Dad had plans for anyone who didn't pass—the fields! Again, that was our motivator!

At the age of 13, I entered **9th grade** as a freshman at Paul Breaux High School, Lafayette, La. In spite of the May 17, 1954, U.S. Supreme Court decision, *Brown v. Board of Education of Topeka, Kansas*, which declared segregation of public schools as unconstitutional and violated the 14th Amendment, segregation continued in the South. Although there was a high school in our hometown of Carencro, it was for "Whites only." Schools, churches, even hospitals were still segregated as well. At the hospitals and clinics, Blacks were seen in one part, the back; Whites were seen up front. Waiting rooms in hospitals and clinics were segregated; Whites entered through the front door while Blacks entered through the back door. Blacks received medical services after the Whites were seen. Water fountains were labeled "White" or "Colored" (that was ours).

High School Years

(blogspot.com)

Although segregated water fountains and restrooms were officially outlawed by the Civil Rights Act of 1964 and signed into law by President Lyndon B. Johnson (July 2, 1964), they yet existed in the south.

(America blog)

In grocery stores, it was not uncommon for a White person to be called to the front of the line and served ahead of Blacks. I recall going to the theater and paying 15 cents to see a movie. Blacks sat upstairs in a limited-seating, over-crowded area, while Whites sat downstairs in a much larger area. From upstairs, some of the Blacks would throw popcorn downstairs at the Whites. I remember one time someone from upstairs poured a drink on the Whites who sat downstairs. The Manager came and made ALL the Blacks leave the theater. We didn't even know who poured the drink, but we had to leave! Yes, we were very upset! That was our movie night!

So, since we couldn't attend the all-White Carencro High School, we would ride the bus from home to Carencro Heights Elementary School in Carencro. We were then "bussed" 7 miles outside the city limits to Paul Breaux High School, an all-Black High School in Lafayette. Paul Breaux High School was the largest school in the Parish. I am grateful for the experience. Here I learned to "change classes." As a Freshman I had about 7 classes and 7 different teachers. At first, I must admit I was scared and intimidated, but my experience in 8th grade coupled with counseling by my teacher and parents helped me to quickly overcome it. Besides, I had two sisters at the same school, so I was fine. All of the Black students from the neighboring towns were bussed to Paul Breaux High School. Lafayette was a "big city" in our eyes. The students had a city mentality; they moved faster! Dating at 12 & 13 and pregnancies at 13 & 14 were not uncommon. They were "different" from us country kids who could not go out without a chaperone or spend the night at our friends' houses or get picked up by boys for a date. It was a "different world from where we came from!"

There were also fights at Paul Breaux High School! I remember standing in line one day, waiting for the teacher to unlock the classroom door. While we waited in line, three inner-city boys jumped one of my classmates who was standing in line just in front of me! They punched him 5 or 6 times, uttered choice words to him and ran off. The students in line just backed away, nobody helped him. I didn't understand "rival groups." Apparently, there was rivalry among some of the athletes from the various towns; it was not uncommon for fights to break out after games. I was never a part of that because we didn't attend games in the evenings. My classmate went home that morning, too embarrassed to return to class. I felt so bad for him! I told my Dad, and his response, "*les les petits kanaigh-la tronkin,*" (leave them bad kids alone; or stay away from them bad kids). Some of the inner-city kids also talked back

High School Years

to the teachers and were not disciplined. But I got used to the environment. I learned at an early age to avoid trouble, stay away from troublemakers, do my schoolwork and respect the teachers.

I didn't know the "ways" of the inner-city kids. One day a so-call friend of mine asked me to "borrow" my gym suit because she had forgotten hers at home. Naïve as I was, I saw no problem with it. I loan her my gym suit. The next day she said she forgot to bring it, so I received a "0" in my gym class that day for not dressing out! The following day she brought me a "stolen" gym suit with another student's name written on back! I told her it was not mine; she insisted "that's the one you loan me." In essence, she stole a gym suit from another student and gave it to me. She kept the one I had loan her. Well, I wasn't a fighter like the inner-city kids; besides, I would only get expelled for fighting and made to stay home and work the fields! I learned a valuable lesson; don't trust the inner-city kids! Luckily, I had two other sisters in High School, so I was able to use one of their gym suits until Mom finally bought me another one and said, "now let em' steal that one and see what happens to you!" (No mercy!)

My freshman year was a turning point in my life in more ways than one. In spite of the racism, we dealt with from the Whites in the community, I faced a somewhat similar challenge with my "Black" Physical Education teacher; the same one who had given me a "0" grade for not dressing out that day. She seemed to "favor" the inner-city students, the more outgoing ones. We referred to them as "fast" back then. Although I was still an honor student, for whatever reason she would not recognize me as such. I remember taking a written test in her class one day and scoring 100. She wrote on my paper "COPIED VERY WELL" and gave me a grade of "C." She accused me of copying off her "favored" student's paper. I went to her after class almost in tears telling her "I studied, I didn't copy." She claimed, "I saw you looking on Anna Bertha's paper," which was a flat-out lie. I had no need to look at another student's paper; I had prepared myself to make an A! She would not budge! I went home crying to Mom and Dad and told them what happened. They felt bad for me, but they were NOT going to drive 7 miles to the school to argue with the teacher about a grade! Dad said, "God don't like ugly; she'll get what's coming to her down the line." Mom said, "What God gave you, no one can take it away; show her you can make more A's." Mom continued, "show her there's plenty more A's where that one came from!" Well, I did just that! But it was still a painful experience for me!

I developed more "secret crushes" in my freshman year, but I was too "slow" for the boys, so I never dated anyone from Lafayette. I resulted to liking the boys from Sunset and Opelousas; they were good dancers! I'd only see them on weekends at Rocket Beach. I finished the 9th grade at Paul Breaux High School, still an honor student in spite of my stumbling block of a PE teacher! I now know as I write this book, that these experiences, these "growing pains," were only preparing me for the next school year, and for life itself! My Dad used to say, "*Sa ki touye pas toi, fais toi plus fort,*" (what doesn't kill you will make you stronger)." I now know also, that if I faint in the day of adversity, my strength is small (Proverbs 24:10). I've learned also that stumbling blocks do make me stronger, and they help build character. I now embrace opposition; it challenges me to make critical decisions and to move to higher grounds. Above all, it reminds me to trust God through it all. It teaches me to have confidence in God, not man.

It was summertime again and as usual, we worked the fields Monday through Saturday and played games with Mom (bingo and card games) and Dad (mostly baseball) on Saturday afternoons. Sometimes we would turn the music on and dance with Dad. Mom wasn't much of a dancer; she just enjoyed watching us have fun dancing with Dad. We went out on Saturday nights and danced some more. We went to church on Sunday mornings and either visited relatives or played games on Sunday afternoons. That was a normal week. At the age of 14, I met a young man from Sunset. I considered myself dating him, but still couldn't go anywhere alone with him; the chaperone rule still applied! So, we'd just meet at Rocket Beach on Saturday nights and dance. We'd call each other on the "party line" and write letters during the week. That was dating at 14! To my teenage audience, remember, "don't awaken love until the time is right" (Song of Solomon 2:7, NIV).

We continued to attend the local Catholic Church in Carencro (for Blacks only). There was a smaller Catholic Church in the farm area where we lived, it was called Prairie Boss. The Priest would come from Carencro to Prairie Boss on Sunday mornings to conduct service. He was so unfit for the job if I do say so myself! He was not friendly and had an unattractive attitude, to say the least. I remember him coming to church one Sunday morning and refusing to minister because the church was too cold, in his opinion! He fussed at the men in the church for not getting there earlier enough to warm up the church. He left us sitting there and didn't conduct service that Sunday. Mom determined then that we would start going to the bigger Catholic Church in Carencro. We were happy. The church was bigger and prettier, and we got to see our school friends! In the Catholic Church we participated in the Sacraments as we became age-appropriate, such as Baptism as a baby, First Communion at age 6-7, and Confirmation as a young teenager. We attended Catechism (Bible study) on Saturday afternoons, where we were taught by Nuns. We learned prayers and the doctrine of the Roman Catholic Church.

In spite of racial segregation in public schools being declared unconstitutional in 1954, the South was slow-moving! However, in the **1966-67** school year, my sister (Joyce), my brother (Black), 6 other friends and I decided that we were going to make history! We were going to be the first Blacks to integrate the all-White Carencro High School! So, at age 14 I enrolled as a sophomore, **10th grade**. This marked the first school year of desegregation at Carencro High School, Carencro, La. Joyce enrolled as a Jr, and Black, a freshman. History was made! However, we were in for a surprise!

BEARS

(Portion of the old Carencro High School, 1969)

The old Carencro High School which we integrated became Carencro Middle School when the new High school was built in Lafayette in 1970.

Although we were acquainted with racism and prejudice, as this was the climate we were growing up in, we were not accustomed to the face-to-face verbal attacks, insults, and blatant disrespect!

High School Years

Many of the students were unashamedly cruel! To many, our first name became "nigger," without apology! Of particular notice was, the lighter-complexioned Blacks were treated better by the White students than the brown or darker-complexioned Blacks. But we were used to it; we had seen the same *ignorance* among Blacks in prior schools! White students refused to sit with us in the cafeteria. Some refused to drink after us at the water fountains. They refused to use the bathroom after a Black student. It wasn't uncommon for White students to literally RUN out of the bathroom if we entered. Ignorance at its best! Sometimes we would enter the cafeteria and find no available tables to sit at. If we sat at the same table with certain White students, they would get up and leave, even if it meant throwing away their food! So, we got smarter; we began to strategize and to "target" the larger tables. The first Black student to get his/her tray of food would proceed to the larger tables. By simply putting our tray on the table, the White students would scatter, thus creating an available table for Black students! 😊. Problem solved! However, not ALL of the White students were prejudice or ignorant, just a large majority, unfortunately.

Not only did we tolerate racism and prejudice (which I now refer to as ignorance) by White students; sadly, a few of the staff had issues with Black students infiltrating their "all-white" environment. This was reflected in their grading of Black students. For example, I decided to apply for membership in the school's "Honor Society" in my sophomore year, which called for a 3.5 or above grade-point-average (GPA). Just prior to the election of students for the Honor Society, I received my report card with a big red "F" as my grade in Home Economics. WHAT??? I thought, this has got to be a mistake! I had previously calculated my grade as an "A," I had scored an "A" on ALL of my exams and had completed ALL school projects. I approached the teacher at the end of class and asked if this was a mistake. She replied, "It is not." I reminded her that I had scored "A" on all of my tests and that I had turned in all of my required recipes and assignments. She replied, "you did not have a file box." She wanted all recipes in a *file box*. Although I had asked Mom and

Dad time and time again for a "file box," there was never time or occasion to get one. So, I submitted all of my recipes, properly and accurately documented, but stapled together. She had not stressed that the file box itself was part of the grade. Sadly, she would not budge! Again, I was devastated, as I forced myself to hold back the tears in her presence. I was wounded and crushed, as this grade disqualified me for the Honor Society. Touché! That was her goal!

I sat quietly on the bus ride after school. I was so hurt, I pretended to be asleep. Upon arriving home, I told the story to Mom as I cried and cried. Mom was angry (at the teacher as well as the system). Dad was in the field and as our custom was, we went out to meet him and worked until sundown. I kept quiet, just wanting the pain of it all to go away. However, Mom would not keep quiet, she told the story to Dad as soon as he arrived home. Upon hearing the story, Dad felt bad that they had NOT gotten me the file box I had been asking for (I think). However, Mom angrily lashed out, "it's not even about a damn file box! They didn't want you sitting on that stage with them white kids."

Dad had a way with words; he wasn't given to fury or long dialogue about such matters. He would say things like, "nothing goes under the stomach of a beast that don't come around its back and bite him!" What he meant was, "what goes around comes around, she'll get hers. God sees everything; God don't like ugly," were among his favorite sayings. He loved to say, "they can't take from you what God gave you; keep doing good" AND, "put it in God's hands." (For more of his sayings and accompanying stories, see *"Like Dad Use to Say,"* written by my sister, Dr. Joyce Robertson, available at Amazon and Barnes & Noble). Mom on the other hand, was a tad bit radical! She would have probably preferred to go to the school and handle the teacher! However, the climate and culture of the day did not lend itself to fair treatment, so, as a family we moved on.

Some of the other Black students experienced some of the same cruelty. My brother John, (nicknamed Black) was the only Black

High School Years

male student in his freshman year, on the once all-White campus. I learned recently that he had bottled-up many of his experiences. My sister and I would share our experiences with each other, and with Mom and Dad. My brother, on the other hand, kept silent about his. He said it would not have made a difference. He shared with me recently how he suffered verbal insults and abuse at the hands of the White students and a few teachers on a *daily* basis. To this day, it is difficult to get him to discuss anything about his first year of high school. Only recently (July 2021) he shared the following dreadful experiences with me.

During his PE class, he would wait for all the White students to get dressed and leave the locker room before he felt safe enough to enter. Consequently, the (prejudice) coach would always mark him late for class. He learned to bring an extra towel with him to the locker room, because the White students would spit on his locker and sometimes place feces on his locker and pad lock. The extra towel was to clean off his locker. In addition, White students would tape signs on his locker stating, "nigger get out of here" ... "nigger you don't belong here" ... "nigger your dead"!!! When I asked him how he dealt with that, he responded, "How could I have taken them seriously? They weren't even grammatically correct, it's "nigger, **you're** dead" not "nigger **your** dead"!!!! Like my Dad, my brother "humorized" the most awful experiences; seems to be a safe coping mechanism.

Although my brother was an honor student who had been skipped a grade in elementary school, one White teacher accused him of cheating on a test and *gave* him a failing grade. He had scored the highest in his entire class. Umnnnn, I'm just now finding out that it didn't happen to only me! She could not conceive the possibility that this "little nigger" was smarter, or had studied harder, than all the White students in the class. So, he had to have cheated! The test was worth 100 points with an essay question worth 10 points. He was the only one who scored 110 points. The teacher wrote on his paper, "110 points ... copied very well ... F". Umnnnnn, the year prior at an all-Black high school my PE teacher had written on my paper, "Copied very well! C". (I suppose she was more generous than the White teacher was with my brother!) The second highest score was 95. When my brother confronted the teacher about his grade, she would not budge. Sarcastically and angrily, he said to her, "I should have at least gotten a 'D' for knowing which answers **not** to copy for that extra 15 points" (Get it?).

Because he had been moved up a grade in elementary school, my brother was younger and smaller in stature than his classmates. For obvious reasons, he would not participate in the traditional "contact" sports such as football, basketball, baseball or socker. In order to get a grade for participation, he hid behind safe positions such as referee or sideline coach, where they had no legitimate reasons to do him harm. Baseball, he told me, seemed safe enough. "I could have dodged a ball if it was thrown at me, and I had a bat in my hand for defense if needed; so, I felt relatively safe." He shared another experience with me, which sort of angered me after all these years! Again, one of which he had kept silent. On the first day of the baseball season (after removing the saliva and excrement from his locker), he proceeded to the baseball field. It was his turn to get up to the plate and bat. He picked a "shiny bat" and intentionally struck out. But ever since then, whenever the White kids would take the equipment to the field, they would always remove the "shiny bat" from the bag and bring the rest of the bats out to the field. They didn't want to touch or to carry the bat that he had used.

One day, he noticed that the entire bag of bats was left in the equipment room. So, from the bag of bats he picked out his "shiny bat" and proceeded toward the baseball field. This consisted of crossing a basketball court and a football field. Prior to arriving at the baseball field, he could hear the White students shouting, "nigger bring the bats!! Nigger bring the bats!!!" (Bear in mind that carrying a bag of 15-20 bats was no easy task, especially for someone of my brother's stature.) As their cries got louder and

High School Years

more offensive, my brother admitted that he was afraid, but the realization that the only bat on the field was in his hands boosted his confidence and gave him courage!

Once he arrived at the fence that separated the baseball field from the football field, he noticed there was a padlock on the gate. He asked the coach for the keys to open the gate; coach said he didn't have them. He instructed my brother to "climb over the fence" like they had. My brother said he knew this was not true, because he could see the keys hanging on the coach's belt. Nevertheless, he began to climb the fence. As he climbed, a white student decided to antagonize him – "Nigger if you come across that fence without those bats, I'm gonna' whoop your ass." The White student proceeded to throw baseballs at the fence where my brother was climbing. One ball actually hit his fingers, but he said he was determined that under no circumstances was he going to release the bat. The coach told my brother to go back to the gym and get the bag of bats. My brother replied, "I will go back and help carry the bats if you send someone to help me."

We weren't too good at disobeying adults! In fact, if we got out of line with an adult, we'd have to face the wrath of Mom and Dad and no doubt receive double punishment! Yet, my brother told the coach no, he was NOT going to do it alone. When my brother said no, the White student said, "Who you think you talking to Lil Nigger?" He threw another ball at my brother and began to aggressively advance toward him. My brother, who was still holding the "only bat" on the field... Well, you know the rest of the story! As the White student approached, my brother swung and hit him with the bat, and he fell. My brother again made history! First fight at Carencro High School since integration! Defending himself, he hit the White student several times with the bat until they were stopped. Surprisingly, the other White students did not jump in to help the White student! The coach then called the campus police and had my brother escorted to the police department. Although he was relieved to see the police arrive, one could not assume that the danger was over. Remember, this was the deep south in the late 60's. Just imagine, A Black boy who had just hit a White boy with a bat, in the back of a police car being escorted by two White policemen! This did not in any way guarantee a positive outcome! Thankfully, he was transported to the police department without further incidence and my Dad was called. My brother said he was more afraid of my Dad than of the White policemen!

He told me how proud he was of my Dad's response when the policemen told him "your son is here because he hit a White boy with a baseball bat." My Dad's response was, "I raise all of my kids to be non-violent, but I also teach them to defend themselves. So, what did the White kid do to 'deserve' getting hit by my son?" When the policemen explained the story, they received from the coach and the other White students, my Dad went to my brother and asked him what happened. Once my brother explained, my Dad went back to the policemen and simply said, "Can you give Mr. 'So-n-So' a call?" My Dad was always dropping names! Whatever the situation, his response was, "Call Mr. So-n-So," and things would get resolved! It wasn't until later on in our adult lives that we realized, "Mr. So-n-So" was oftentimes the State Representative, US Senator, City Councilman, or *someone* in authority! In dire situations, "Mr. So-n-So" was the Governor!!! He would oftentimes tell us, "It's not always *what* you know that matters, it's *who* you know." After a few phone calls, my brother and my Dad were on their way home.

Well, my brother was expelled from school for a week. My Mom's response, "next time hit him in the head with the bat!" Sorry, it was just an expression stemming from frustration and anger. My brother said he thought about quitting school at this point; but this would have resulted in him working the fields with Dad. Since that was not an option for him, he opted to return to school and continue to endure. To this day he tells me, "A lesser man would

High School Years

have required 'decades' of therapy to get past his first year of high school!"

Academically, all nine of us Black students fared well that first year, despite the prejudice, verbal abuse, maltreatment, snickering, degradation and mere ugliness of many! However, we were a determined group, destined to succeed, and we did!

Well, by that time I "considered" myself dating. I had met a young man from Sunset at the dance; Sunset is a small, neighboring city. He was a good dancer. I seemed to be attracted to good dancers because I was one 😊. Then came the Lent season, mid-March to early-April. In the Catholic Church, Lent is considered a "fasting" season; we didn't go out during this season. I had heard rumors that he had begun dating a student at his school. So, when I returned to Rocket Beach after the Lent season, there he was with his "new girlfriend." So, I experienced heart break for the first time; at least that's what I thought it was. His newfound relationship was short-lived, and he tried to make his way back to me, but the door was closed! I moved on. I met another young man from Opelousas, another good dancer. That was short lived. I found out I was a year older than him, and it didn't sit right with me; I lost interest. Oh, these teenage years of mine! Frivolous they may have been, but part of the growing process.

The following school year, 1967-1968, my junior year, **11th grade,** more Blacks registered at Carencro High School. In fact, a few of the Black students joined the football team. They were great players, so the coach welcomed them. Fortunately, the coach wanted to win so he gave them lots of playing time. The maltreatment from some of the White students (and teachers) declined, but unfortunately continued; ignorance is bliss to some!

Life on the farm continued as usual. School Monday-Friday, work in the fields after school, take baths, eat dinner, do homework, recite prayers, and go to bed. On weekends, play games with the neighborhood friends or go fishing and hunting with Dad, go out on Friday or Saturday night, church on Sunday, visit relatives (or they would visit us on Sunday afternoons), and back to school on Monday. That was the norm. So, I met another good dancer from Opelousas. We courted for a short while, the latter part of my high school years. However, being from Opelousas, we only saw each other on weekends. My sister Joyce dated his friend. Dad and Mom had become a little less strict on us girls, as all the chaperones had moved on. So, we were allowed to go out without chaperones, but still had curfew! And no drinking! Occasionally the boyfriends would drive by the house during the week, but Dad put a stop to that! We were working girls; they were city boys. However, he allowed them to come by on weekends.

My high school years were rather tumultuous! Coupled with challenges of school integration (where we were not welcomed) were the Selma and Montgomery, Alabama marches led by Dr. Martin Luther King Jr. Dr. King led non-violent marches throughout the south, protesting racial inequalities and harsh treatment of Blacks and other minorities.

"Segregation in the South, 1956." Photography archive – The Gordan Parks Foundation (gordonparksfoundation.org)

The protesters experienced cruelty by the police department during these non-violent marches. Loosing of bull dogs, use of opened fire hydrants on the marchers, and beatings with bats and clubs were common practices of the policemen. Many of the marchers were jailed and faced charges during these non-violent marches.

"Segregation in the South, 1956." Photography archive – The Gordan Parks Foundation (gordonparksfoundation.org)

Racial tension was at such a peak that uneasiness was felt throughout the nation, including our classrooms. White students said horrible things; Black students retaliated. Fights began at our high school in our second year of integration and grew considerably in the third year! The assassination of Dr. Martin Luther King Jr. on April 4, 1968, and of Presidential Candidate Robert F. Kennedy on June 5, 1968, increased racial tension and riots in the South. The nation was in turmoil! Upon the death of Dr. Martin Luther King Jr., one of the White students in my class laughingly shouted out "they finally got him! They finally got that nigger!" The teacher *reluctantly* corrected him, as she began to instruct the class. My sister's teacher was considerate enough to have her classroom pause for a moment of silence. A White student in her class asked, "what if we don't want to pray?" The teacher responded, "then pray for yourself!"

Ethel Morale Gathers

Yes, tensions continued in the classrooms as well as on the school bus. One morning it was raining as we waited for the school bus. Rather than stand in the rain at the bus stop, we waited until the bus drove past our house, made a U-turn at the end of the road and returned. As it was approaching, we began to run in the rain toward the bus stop. The school bus driver (an elderly White man) looked at us and without hesitation kept on going! He did not wait at the bus stop for us. We missed school that day, the neighbors' kids as well. The very next day the same bus driver arrived at one of the White high-school students' home. The students Mom came to the door and asked, "can you give her 5 more minutes, she's not quite ready?" The bus driver replied "ok" and actually WAITED for the student. Well, here was my opportunity to get into trouble and I took it, "sassing a White man." I said out loud "oh, he couldn't wait for us in the rain yesterday, but he can wait for the White girl." He said, "*qui to dire t-neg?*" (What did you say lil' nigger?) I had the audacity to loudly repeat, "I SAID YOU COULDN'T WAIT FOR US YESTERDAY, AND IT WAS RAINING, BUT YOU CAN WAIT FOR THE WHITE GIRL TO COME OUT OF HER HOUSE!" He had the nerve to respond, "Mais I gotta' wait for her, that's my granddaughter." Well, I was already in trouble for "sassing a White man" so I kept going, "I DON'T CARE IF SHE'S YOUR GRAND-DAUGHTER! YOU COULD HAVE WAITED FOR US YESTERDAY! YOU SAW US RUNNING IN THE RAIN! BUT YOU KEPT ON GOING!" He told me to shut my mouth! "*Bouch ta jell T-Neg!*" (Shut your mouth lil nigger). I replied "NO! YOU ARE WRONG!" Well, you could have heard a pin drop on the bus; it was quiet the rest of the way to school! It didn't end there.

While sitting in my first period classroom, I was summoned to the principal's office. I arrived at the office only to see the bus driver sitting in the principal's office. The principal asked me what happened, and I told him. Without hesitation, he instructed me to apologize to the bus driver for disrespecting him. I refused to apologize (principally based stubbornness), insisting that what the bus driver did was WRONG. The conclusion of the matter, I got

High School Years

suspended from riding the school bus for a week. Mom picked me up from school and upon hearing the story she consoled me. Of course, Dad said I was wrong in talking back and I should have apologized! Mom said I did right; hence the difference between Dad and Mom's counsel. Dad was the peacemaker, Mom was the "enough is enough" kind of lady! No nonsense! Mom drove me to school the rest of the week. I was glad; it was good quality time with Mom 😊. While I am not advocating that children "mouth-off" at adults and feel justified, I share this truth merely to add another "glimpse" of the unpleasantry of racial tension and inequality. The process of integration was not a pleasant experience. However, we learned to adjust to the racial climate, some more grudgingly than others.

By this time, the Blacks at Carencro High School had multiplied in number, enough to decide "we're not taking this anymore." There were fights, and more fights. I remember particularly when a fight broke out among the male students, Blacks against Whites, behind a quarrel that apparently started on the football field and was not resolved. It was horrible! Approximately 20 students were involved. Many received suspensions for "starting and provoking" the fight, others, for engaging. Even with the suspensions, tension continued. I can honestly say the White students gradually stopped "picking" on the Black students. The *new* Black students were not as pleasant or tolerant as the nine of us who initially integrated the school. Therefore, tension, racial slurs and discrimination gradually subsided. However, sad to admit, though there was no outward display, racism was yet imbedded in the hearts of many then, and still is today!

By my senior year of high school (1968-1969), **12th grade,** tension had declined. Fights were pretty much non-existent. The Black population had increased to approximately one-fourth of the school population. The all-Black Paul Breaux High School in Lafayette had been totally shut down and now Blacks had no choice but to attend the White high schools in their community, including the once all-White, Carencro High School. Senior year was pretty much "smooth sailing" especially for those who had already met the graduation requirements. Many of the White students were eating at the same tables with the Black students, so progress had been made. As we approached graduation practice, I was about to enter places I had never stepped in before. A Catholic service was scheduled for Seniors at the "All-White" Catholic Church. As we entered the Church for practice, I thought, "Wow, such an upgrade from our All-Black Catholic Church!" Then we proceeded to the Cajun Dome where the graduation ceremony would be held, again, a first time for me. Of course, today everything is integrated, but as stated before, in spite of desegregation laws passed, the south was slow-moving, even in the 20th Century!

Teachers were less "openly" prejudice, but a few still found subtle ways to keep Blacks out of the Honor Society! It's as though Whites could not accept the fact that "some" Black students were smarter than "some" White students! I can recall a so-called counseling session with one of my teachers who asked me what were my plans upon graduation. I replied, "I want to go to college and become a teacher." She replied, "I don't think teaching is the field for you; you should probably consider becoming a librarian or secretary." Well, that ended my career counseling sessions! She could not dream with me! Rather, she could not see me doing her job! I knew scholarships and grants were out of the question, so I turned my heart elsewhere and began to consider other career goals.

The Air Force recruiter came to our school one day. I took the information down and told him I was interested in the Air Force. My sister Joyce had joined the year prior and was loving it. She convinced me to join. So, I filled out the application. Mom didn't want my sister and I to leave home, but Dad said, "we've done our part in raising them, you have to let them go!" (Thanks Dad!) I took the test for the Air Force and did very well. Later I took the medical exam and passed that also. Interestingly, the Air Force flew me from Lafayette to New Orleans to the Military Entrance Processing

High School Years

Station (MEPS) to take the physical exam. I had never flown before. I had never been to New Orleans before. I had never stayed in a hotel before. A young, naïve, little country girl, all alone in the city of New Orleans in a hotel, the Sheraton! Culture shocked within my own state! I had never been out of the state, with the exception of the periodic 2-hour rides to Beaumont, TX with my parents. I was all alone and afraid in the hotel room. I slept with the lamp on. I think my Dad was equally afraid! He never let us go to the Mardi-Gras parades in New Orleans. He always said, "New Orleans is not a place for you; it's a dangerous city." So, I was afraid of New Orleans.

Well, I passed the medical exam and upon returning home I enlisted in the "Delayed Entry Program," meaning that upon completion of high school and upon my 18th birthday, I could enter the United States Air Force (USAF). I did this in my Senior year. I couldn't wait to tell the teacher who told me to consider becoming a librarian or secretary that I had enlisted in the United States Air Force! She could only wish me well when she learned of my new career plan.

Then came graduation!
High School Graduation, 1969

The valedictorian and salutatorian (White students) represented the class by addressing the class and audience on the night of graduation. We had attended the White Catholic Church only to be stared at; they were not accustomed to seeing Blacks in the all-White Church. We experienced the same at the Cajun Dome. Then it was all over. I did not attend the high school prom that year; I was not interested! I had made it through the cruelty of three high school years and experienced injustices by faculty and students! I had enough. I was also discouraged from enrolling in college. I just wanted to leave Carencro!

After high school graduation, I spent six months at home. I graduated in June 1969 at the age of 17 but had to wait until my 18th birthday (November) to enter the Air Force. Looking back, I'm thankful for those six months I spent at home with Dad, Mom, my three younger brothers and my first cousin, Linda. Mom had rescued Linda at the age of three, taken her under her wings 10 years prior, and raised her as her own! Linda had become a "little sister" to me. Of course, they went to school during the day; so, I was left alone with Dad to work the fields. I'm thankful for the time of bonding even more with my Mom and Dad during these six months. I'm thankful for the "life lessons" Dad taught me while I listened to his corny jokes in the field. He truly was a jokester! By then Dad was farming less. All of my older siblings had gone from home to pursue their own careers. The younger ones were not very good in the field, according to Dad. They hated it, so they frustrated Dad.

By then Dad and Mom were a little bit more lenient with me (than they had been with my 5 older sisters). I could actually go to friend's houses on weekends and go out with them without a chaperon! There were no more chaperones in the house! I still had curfews though! I even got to spend half the summer with my oldest sister, Eva, in Beaumont. She introduced me to this young man, a co-worker of hers. He was nice. He liked me. He was different. He couldn't dance very well but he was a "good person," respectful, had a job, and had his own car. I went to a drive-in movie with him one night. My FIRST TIME going out with a boy by

High School Years

myself! 17 years old! He was generous and respectful and paid for my movie and popcorn. He knew I was leaving for the Air Force upon returning home to La. So, at the end of the summer he gave me a "promise ring" and talked about getting married someday. HUH? Marriage? I was NOT ready for that! This was my first taste of freedom, and I was not going to mess it up! I was SET on joining the Air Force. We wrote to each other for a year or so but moved on.

I later learned from my brother Black when he graduated from high school the following year (1970), that the rules for the graduating class in Carencro had changed. The faculty decided that THEY would represent the graduating class with speeches on graduation night instead of the valedictorian and salutatorian, as was the custom. You see, the class of 1970 had a *Black* valedictorian and a *Black* salutatorian. The same thing happened the following year (1971), with Black students placing at the head of the class. I thought back to the words spoken by my Mom, "they can't accept the fact that some Black students are smarter than some White students." Perhaps there was truth in it! However, I spoke with my niece recently whose three children have graduated from the new, fully integrated Carencro High School. She stated, "it's not that way anymore; the valedictorian this year was Black, and he gave a speech at the graduation ceremony." I don't know when the rule changed, but it certainly was the right thing to do!

CARENCRO HIGH SCHOOL - LAFAYETTE, LA.

Ethel Morale Gathers

A new Carencro High School was built in 1970-1971 in Lafayette, La. after my brother Black and I graduated. It is one of six Lafayette Parish public high schools. Minority population of the school is at 73%. It is my desire that the current minority students appreciate the work of us trailblazers, that they would understand the privileges and treatment afforded to them today was paved by their predecessors: Blacks in the graduating classes of 1968-1970. Make us proud!

Lafayette, La.

CHAPTER 7

Military Service

On December 5, 1969, I entered the United States Air Force at the age of 18 and headed to Basic Training at Lackland AFB (LAFB), San Antonio, TX. It was my ticket off the farm! I arrived at the San Antonio International Airport, having absolutely no idea where Lackland Air Force Base was. It dawned on me that I was quickly GROWING UP! No Dad, no Mom, no big brother/big sister, no teacher, no Nun, no chaperon to guide or watch over me; I was on my own! Luckily, there were Technical Instructors (TIs) from the Base to meet us at the airport. There were others my age who were joining the Air Force as well. Together we boarded the bus with a couple of TI's and headed to Lackland.

Upon arrival at the training area of the Base, it became real! The "nice" Technical Instructors who greeted us at the airport put on their TI hats and suddenly they were transformed! "OFF THE BUS, NOW! MOVE IT! MOVE IT! GET YOUR LUGGAGE AND LINE UP AGAINST THE WALL! LET'S GO! LET'S GO! NOW! …. I wondered if those were the same people who met us at the airport! Fortunately, my sister Joyce had been through basic training and warned me of what to expect, so, I was not surprised. Also, coming from a strict home, obedience was not an option. Therefore, listening to Technical Instructors was not a problem! The yelling continued, as we were assigned rooms and roommates in the

Military Service

dormitories and instructed, "NO TALKING!" You could only hear the hustle and bustle noise of suitcases being moved around. The fairness of basic training is everyone is treated the same! No partiality. No favoritism. Though there were girls from all across the country, we were yet all "Airmen." As the yelling continued from day to day, I pretty much accepted that this is how it was going to be for the next 6 weeks of my life! But I was disciplined, and was determined to make it through, as my sister Joyce had.

Training was rigorous and very much regimented. Everything we did was on schedule. Up at 5:00 AM, showers at a certain time, formation at a certain time, meals at a certain time, classes at a certain time, physical activity at a certain time—all accompanied with the yelling of Technical Instructors. We marched and sang cadence everywhere we went. I must admit, annoying as it may have been, discipline was always "constructive." We learned from our mistakes and became better Airmen. I can recall getting yelled at for forgetting my name tag one morning. As we stood in formation and was inspected by the TI, she spared me no embarrassment. She lectured me LOUDLY in front of the entire Flight. I was subsequently assigned the extra duty of "name tag monitor" for the remainder of Basic Training. I had to be in formation earlier than everyone else, as it became my duty to check everyone for name tags before the TI's came to inspect us. Lesson learned: I never forgot my name tag again! I recall also the Airmen who responded "ok" to a TI instead of "Yes Ma'am." She was instructed to go to the latrine (bathroom, that is) at the end of the hallway and "flush OK down the toilet." The Airmen had to yell "OK" and flush, "OK" and flush, "OK" and flush, until told to stop. Lesson learned: she never responded "ok" to a TI for the remainder of Basic Training!

Basic training was definitely a learning experience! Some did not make it due to lack of discipline, medical issues, inability to adapt, or some other reason. So, in mid-January 1970, I graduated from Basic Training.

**Basic Training Graduation
Lackland AFB (1970)**

Upon graduation from Basic Training, I proceeded to my first duty assignment, Charleston AFB, S.C. Here, I experienced my first real job at the age of 18, Telephone Switchboard Operator. I had never worked outside the fields of Louisiana. I excelled at my job. Dad and Mom had instilled in us the will to do and to be our best at whatever we pursued. I had scored pretty high on the Armed Services Vocational Aptitude Battery (ASVAB), so I was placed in a technical field, Communications Center Specialist, a 24-hour operation. The Switchboard was where they started everyone in this specialty prior to moving them to the Communications Center. I would work three different shifts diligently, as scheduled, and party on weekends! Here was my first *real* taste of freedom, no permission necessary! Well, to an extent that is, because we still had curfew and the doors of the dormitory were locked at a certain time. We were required to sign in and out of the dormitory, and we dare not miss curfew!

Military Service

I had never been to Charleston, SC, so, I was out to explore every facet of the city. I gained new friends. We would drive off base on weekends and tour the city and surrounding areas. After all, I had "joined the Air Force to see the world!" That was the Air Force's motto to attract recruits. The city of Charleston had many attractions. Just to name a few: the Battery, the Charleston boat tours, The Isle of Palms Country Park, the Charleston walking tours, Folly Beach, the Museums, Ft. Sumpter National Monument, the Citadel, the Plantation Historic Sites and many, many more! Charleston is located on the waterfront, so seafood was plentiful! If you are a lover of seafood, Charleston is the place to visit. A favorite pastime was to attend an oyster-bake on weekends, where crab-boils and shrimp were also plentiful. The music and entertainment were also great, consisting of live bands, just like home in Louisiana. My friends and I would go out on weekends and still go to church "somewhere" on Sunday mornings. One of my friends was Baptist, two were Pentecostal, and I was Catholic. What a motley crew we were! We were all brought up in church, two of them were daughters of Pastors. We would rotate visiting each other's denominational church on Sunday mornings. This was also a learning curve for me! I was not familiar with any churches besides the Roman Catholic Church.

I dated, but it was difficult to establish long-lasting relationships due to rotations, permanent changes of station, or people simply exiting the military! People completed their tour of duty sometimes within one to two years and were moved to other locations. I dated this guy in my Unit, but after about 7 months he exited the military and moved back home to New York. We communicated for a short while, but then moved on. At the end of a year and a half, I met this gentleman that I became very fond of. He was a school teacher and he talked me into taking college classes. I had been scorned by the teachers and counselors in the predominately white schools in La. I didn't want to repeat the experience! However, he talked me into enrolling in *one* class to try it out. I admired his maturity and intelligence, plus he was tall and handsome!

So, I enrolled in an English class. He introduced me to a colleague and friend of his, an English Professor. I had written a paper in my class titled, "The Creole Dialect of Louisiana." His friend reviewed my paper and made a few edits. I was so proud of my paper, written strictly from experience. The English Teacher graded my paper and gave me the grade of "C." I was crushed! Here we go again! I approached her about my grade, and she replied, "sounds like it came straight out the dictionary!" The problem was, she could not find any mistakes on my paper! Well, my experiences at the all-White high school in Carencro, La. had prepared me for this! The teachings of my parents had also prepared me for this. I knew I had to keep going; quitting was not an option! So, I stopped letting his friend proof my writings. The following semester I enrolled in two classes, and it grew from there. Within a year of dating this gentleman I received orders to Japan. We kept in touch for a while, but soon thereafter went our separate ways. By then I was 20 years old, with marriage nowhere in view.

In-between assignments I went home on 30-days leave. My Mom and Dad were ever so proud of me, just as they had been when my sister, Joyce, had come home in uniform. Mom and Dad asked me to wear my uniform EVERYWHERE! They took me to visit grandparents, uncles and aunts, distant relatives and friends, in uniform. Oh, let's not forget church, I wore the uniform to church! Mom and Dad asked lots of questions about the Air Force and encouraged me again to do my best. I didn't return to visit my high school. Looking back, I probably should have, but I had no desire.

After 30 days at home, I left for Japan. Very scarry experience I must say—new place, new culture, new language. I grew up quickly in Japan. At the age of 20, I arrived at the Tokyo International Airport, Tokyo, Japan. However, my assignment was to Misawa, Japan, 500 miles north of Tokyo. Not knowing the language, I had

Military Service

to seek someone (anyone) who spoke the English language to find out how to get from Tokyo to Misawa. There was no airport in Misawa. I learned that I had to travel by train to get there. Now, how do I get to the train station from the airport? One Japanese gentleman who spoke the English language fluently was kind enough to escort me to a cab driver and told him to take me to the train station. What an experience! I was scared, but inwardly I prayed for God's protection, and He did just that! I arrived at the train station and managed to purchase a ticket to Misawa, Japan. Thank God for the Japanese man being fluent in English!

I had never ridden a train before, another "first time" experience. The train ride itself was long and scarry! I was the only Black person on the train and the further North we traveled, the more stares I received. I began to have flashbacks of the racism in La. But through prayer, I was able to dismiss my thoughts and fears and focus on the fact that I was in Japan, headed to my duty station! I had joined the Air Force and now I was seeing the world! Yes, I was growing up fast! Finally, upon arrival at the Misawa train station, I was told to catch a cab to the Air Base. When I finally arrived at my duty station, Misawa AB, Japan, I was so exhausted, but RELIEVED! It was snowing and freezing cold, another first! I had never lived in snowy and icy climates before! What an experience just to get there! Yet I found my way, got climatized, and later learned enough words in the Japanese language to get around on and off the Base.

I learned my new job and excelled, always remembering the work ethics of my Dad and the teachings of my Mom to "do my best." I received promotions on time. I gained new friends, two of which I am still in contact with today, Georgia and Gloria. Good friendships are to be valued and not to be taken for granted. I connected with beautiful families and started attending the Chaplain services on Base. I met a young man who was a Mason. He introduced me to an organization called "Eastern Star," an American organization abroad. The Masons were an organization of men only, while the Eastern Star were an organization of women only. I didn't quite understand the constitution of the organizations because they were so "secretive." But I figured the works they did were good works. They sponsored activities and fund raisers to assist young airmen and their families; they granted scholarships to graduating high school students; they visited the orphanage in Japan and spent time with the children; and they were members of the Base Chapel choir, just to name a few. So, I found myself supporting their activities, though I never joined as a member. It wasn't long before the Eastern Star members convinced my friends and me to join the gospel choir. I had not been a member of any choir since my younger days in the Catholic Church back home. So, two of my friends and I joined. We enjoyed the fellowship and the family-type environment it created for us single girls away from home.

I enjoyed walking downtown in Japan, enjoying the culture and the food. One of my favorite pastimes was to visit the tailor shops and have clothes made. Tailor shops were abundant! All we needed was a picture or idea of what we wanted made. We would choose our fabric; the tailors would take our measurements and make it— designer clothes with our name sewn into the garments. That was fun! I still have a couple of outfits that I kept (as souvenirs). Skiing was the #1 sport, but I never learned to ski. I saw too many Americans with broken legs and on crutches due to skiing! However, I joined Japan's Volleyball Team and played against teams throughout the Pacific. Hawaii was the force to recon with; they were unbeatable. Of course, they practiced year-round! We took 2nd place to them in the Pacific Air Force tournaments. Another hobby was to attend Japanese festivals. One year the Base was invited to participate. A couple of my friends and I dared to accept the invitation! We enjoyed practicing the dances with the Japanese citizens, and on the day of the festival we put on our "kimono dresses" and danced with them. We had a great time; and did I say the foods were great?

Military Service

Japanese Festival, Misawa, Japan (1972)

Well, I heard from the gentleman I had been acquainted with in S.C. He wanted to know if I was taking college classes. I was not. I was just having a great time! So, he convinced me to go to the Education office on Base, and the rest is history. I enrolled with St. Mary's University and took classes the entire length of my tour, while yet enjoying sight-seeing, shopping, dating, partying, church activities, and concerts. That seemed to be what most people did! He informed me that he had re-entered the military. He had previously served 6 years and gotten out. He also informed me that his duty assignment would be Norton AFB, Ca. upon completion of his technical training. As a little girl, I had always dreamed of going to California! I dreamed of going to Hollywood and meeting movie stars. I pictured myself as one of the Beverly Hillbillies leaving country life and having no clue of city life! But I still dreamed of going there. My 18-months tour of duty was about to end in Japan. I was prepared to say farewell to all of my friends and acquaintances. It had been a wonderful and fun tour of duty. At the end of my assignment in Japan, I reenlisted and got stationed at Norton AFB, in San Bernardino, CA. Coincidence?

Well, I was nowhere near Hollywood, but I got to visit, and to my surprise, I saw no movie stars! They didn't come out and walk the streets as I expected, plus I was about 2 hours away, depending on traffic! So, I settled for visiting the museums and seeing wax sculptures of movie stars and entertainers. I visited the amusement parks and enjoyed going to football games and concerts in Los Angeles. I was also reacquainted with the gentleman from S.C. for another year and a half, then he was re-assigned to Korea, a remote tour, an "unaccompanied" tour.

My life began to unravel at the age of 23. By now I'm considering marriage, but unsure. Too much time, distance, and uncertainties to deal with, so we tabled it. To complicate matters, I was dealing with an unplanned pregnancy. Oh no! I was confused, ashamed and afraid. Though it was widely accepted, especially in California, it was yet taboo in the Catholic Church, a disgrace to my parents, and a scar to myself and my career. Yet there was somewhat of a feeling of gladness, fulfilling my desire to become a mother. I was perplexed; abortion was not an option for me. So, I decided, I'm doing this! I'm going through with this pregnancy and I'm having this baby. I decided I'm staying in the Air Force, and I'll be just fine! However, my life continued to unravel as I progressed in the pregnancy, became ill and had to be hospitalized just prior to his departure for Korea. Before he shipped out, he drove to Louisiana. and picked up my Mom and brought her to Ca. He informed her that I was hospitalized (but didn't tell her why), and that he was being shipped out to Korea in a few days. His final words to me before departure, "I love you, and name that boy Regis." He had selected the name. Then off to Korea he went; he shipped out in the 8th month of my pregnancy.

Military Service

I had developed a condition known as pre-eclampsia, also called toxemia (blood poisoning by toxins from a local bacterial infection). Pre-eclampsia is associated with high blood pressure, protein in urine, and swelling in legs, feet and ankles. Unfortunately, I had all of the above. I had kept this pregnancy in secrecy from my family. I was dealing with it alone, not wanting to disappoint anyone or having anyone feel sorry for me. I was strong and I was going to deliver this baby boy alone, so I thought. However, prognosis was poor, for myself and for my unborn child. After a week's hospitalization, the Doctors determined it best to induce labor, as the condition had worsened. I overheard one of the doctors from the hallway saying, "your daughter is very sick." Mom had made her way to the hospital; The Dr. was briefing her on my condition.

When Mom walked in my hospital room, our eyes met. I can't even begin to explain my feelings at that moment; sickly, ashamed and sorrowful, but at the same time relieved and glad at the sight of my Mom. She was such a strong woman, having delivered 15 babies herself and having lost three due to complications. Who better to understand what I was going through! She said to me, *"pran kouraj"* (take courage), as she leaned across my hospital bed, hugged and kissed me. Those two words spoke volumes! They were so comforting to me. No condemnation, no lecture, just encouraging words. (Somehow Mom knew my condition prior to her arrival). I was so happy and blessed to have my Mom at my side. Mom was a great comfort; don't know how I would have made it without her. I must admit I didn't know how to lean on the Lord then to be my Rock, my Comforter, my Strength…. so, I leaned on Mom. She only spoke words of encouragement to me.

I learned of another complication called "nuchal cord," the umbilical cord wrapped around the baby's neck 360 degrees! The medical profession was not as advanced then as it is today. Procedures are being done today which were non-existent in the mid-70's. This condition, coupled with the induction of labor, hypertension and all of the other complications caused loss of oxygen to my unborn child. Howbeit, I delivered a beautiful 4 lbs. 8 oz baby boy and named him Regis Alan Gathers. This was the happiest day of my life! Yet, little did I know I was about to undergo the most traumatic experience of my lifetime. My beautiful baby boy had encountered a life-threatening condition during the birth process: necrotizing enterocolitis (death of intestinal tissue) due to lack of oxygen. On the third day, he underwent surgery, but passed away due to this condition.

Words cannot express the excruciating, inscrutable, piercing pain that the death of a child brings! I had never experienced such degree of pain in my life! It's as though I had lost my will to live. I'm so thankful to God that my Mom was at my side. I didn't really know how to "look unto the hills from whence cometh my help" (Ps 121:1), but I surely knew how to look to Mom for courage, strength, and the right words at the right time! She was my strength!

Mom remained with me in California during my entire six-weeks convalescent period, carrying me through the days ahead. Afterwards, she wanted to take the bus back to LA; She would not fly! She was of the "if God wanted me to fly, He would have given me wings" generation. However, I talked her into returning home by train. She returned home and bragged to her sisters, cousins and friends that she had been to California to visit me; never really told them *"why."* How I thank my God for the wonderful Mom He blessed me with!

So, I returned to work and continued my career with the Air Force. I struggled mentally through the days ahead, but somehow managed to refocus and to set my sight on my educational goal. This time I went to the Education Office on my own and registered for classes. I had become a very good student with graduation in view. I was also invited to church by a co-worker, Technical Sergeant Albert Thomas, who remains my friend today. He had a beautiful family, wife and five kids. They were from Louisiana,

Military Service

which also bonded us together. I became attached to them. I needed "family" so badly, and they became exactly that to me. They belonged to a Pentecostal church, Church of God in Christ, to be exact. I attended service with him and his family one Sunday, and it was a turning point in my life! New religion, new Church culture. I marveled at their knowledge and love for the Word of God, the Bible, of which I was not very well acquainted. Though I was raised in church, I was not accustomed to studying independently and memorizing scripture. I was not taught to develop a relationship with God. I gained new friends in this church. I accepted Jesus Christ as my Lord and Savior and I received the Baptism of the Holy Spirit. This may be foreign language to many, yet it's an experience that I encourage all of my family members and readers to seek (Read the Book of Acts in the Bible, Chapter 2).

Well in a nutshell, I married the gentleman from S.C. a year after his return from Korea and became Mrs. Richard Alan Gathers. No elaborate expenditures or big extravagant wedding, but a simple, private wedding. Weeping may endure for a night, but joy comes in the morning (Psalm 30:5)! My mourning was turned into joy when I gave birth to a beautiful baby girl a few years later. We named her Nathasha Lynette, nicknamed Nat, weighing 8 lbs., 14 oz. I named her after a friend of my husband's family whom I had met in Charleston years prior. I loved that name the moment I heard it; I saved it for that moment. Nat brought much joy in our lives; it was fascinating to watch her grow. She was dedicated in the Church of God in Christ, while my friends, Albert and Geraldine (Geri) Thomas, who had introduced me to the ways of the Lord, stood as Godparents. The military awarded me 30 days of convalescence leave. What a blessing to be home with my baby. I'm thankful to Geri, Godmother and friend; she became my babysitter when I returned to work. I couldn't stand to be away from my baby! I'd call Geri on every break just to check on her, until finally she said, "Ethel, if you call here one more time, I'm not answering the phone; your baby is fine." So, back to work I went, learning to trust my baby in the hands of another. And it worked out just fine! I couldn't have asked for a better sitter.

I loved my job at Norton AFB. My supervisors were all good, family-oriented people. They cared for my progression and my career. Under their leadership and tutelage, I gained another promotion, to Staff Sergeant, which was difficult in the Communications field. But I did it! Work was good. Church was good. Life was good. Meanwhile, my husband was reassigned to S.C. for a year, and I was left a single parent working rotating shifts. Military life is not always conducive to family life! Rotating shifts involved working swing shift from 4-12 PM, midnight shift from 12 midnight to 8 AM, and day shift from 8:00 AM to 4:00 PM, then 2 days off. I struggled, in more ways than one! Adjusting to marriage, parenthood, and complicated work schedules brought about a serious challenge that we were not prepared for. Therefore, I decided to change career field and I cross-trained into the Military Personnel Field which offered better hours, 7:30 AM to 4:30 PM Mon-Fri, off on weekends and Holidays. It was more conducive for family life. Again, I thank God for my sister, Eva, who kept Nat (4 months old) for two months while I trained at Keesler AFB in Biloxi, MS.

Military Service

It was hard not seeing my baby, but I stayed focused, knowing the decision I was making was for the betterment of my family and career. I graduated with Honors from the Military Personnel School, returned to Beaumont to get my baby and returned to CA. I'm grateful for my church family and friends, my support system in time of need. I also grew in the Lord, learning and memorizing Bible verses, going to church functions, and living a good life!

A year later my husband and I were reassigned to Holloman AFB, Alamogordo, New Mexico. We had to get use to cold climate again, snowing, and waking up to freezing cars in the mornings. We lived in the mobile home park on Base, no garage. In the mornings my husband shoveled snow and pre-heated our cars for at least 10 minutes before going to work. Thank God again for a Godly, Christian woman (Sister Edwards) that I met in base housing who became my babysitter for Nat. She was the perfect sitter. Again, I am grateful. New Mexico was not the best assignment for us. My supervisors and upline did not compare to the caring family of Supervisors I had in CA. My husband was not too enchanted with his job either. This along brought challenges! The base is located in the desert, 89 miles from El Paso and 68 miles from Las Cruces. An attraction would be to visit the white sands 17 miles away or drive 89 miles to El Paso to visit the mall. Unfortunately, there were not many attractions there in the 1970's.

Approximately a year after settling in New Mexico, Darryl and Michael, my husband's twin sons came to live with us at the age of 10. It was a growing experience for me, as I was so accustomed to having one child only for 18 months, now I'm gaining two stepsons, 10 years of age. Fortunately, they were not bad boys. They were easy to live with and very respectful. They embraced Nat, whom they had never met, and Nat loved her big brothers. We enrolled them in school on Base and got them involved in sports. They adapted very well. It was a new day for me; attending sports games at an elementary school, but it was fun. We grew together as a family.

Upon completion of his enlistment, my husband exited the military (again) and took a position in San Antonio, TX where my sister (Joyce) and her family were stationed. At the end of my tour of duty, after 8 years of active military service, I exited the military as well, and joined him in San Antonio.

U.S.A.F. (1977)

I decided to focus on completing my degree. It was time! I enlisted in the Air Force Reserves at Kelly Air Force Base in San Antonio, working one weekend per month and two weeks active duty per year.

Military Service

Civil Service - Kelly AFB/Lackland AFB

After settling down in San Antonio, Texas I became a homemaker, a stay-at-home Mom for the first time; I took a year off from the workforce. I enjoyed every minute of being at home with my then 2-year-old daughter, Nat, while the boys attended the local public school. After a year, I decided to return to the workforce. I sought employment with the federal government and was hired in a civil service position as a File Clerk at Kelly Air Force Base. I was told by a few fiends that I had to "get my foot in the door" if I wanted to work civil service. So, I accepted this position and worked in the Technical Order library. My main responsibility was to maintain current technical orders, instructions and manuals for the pilots. The orders governed particular aircrafts and were very crucial to the mission. I liked my job and excelled in it.

My family experienced tragedies between the years of 1978-1981. In 1978, while employed at Kelly AFB, I received a devastating call one night from my oldest sister, Eva. She was calling to inform me of the death of our sister, Ella, who was 31 years old. It was reported to the family that Ella had been murdered, and her husband was a suspect and had been arrested. Again, this devastated the family. She was the first of 12 siblings to pass through the door of death. Mom and Dad were devastated, so we did all that was necessary to hold together as a family and to support our parents in this loss. Ella had 4 children, ranging between the ages of 2-9. They had been placed in State custody. However, when Mom and Dad requested custody of the four, the children were released to them. They took my two nieces and two nephews to the farm in La. to avoid placement in foster care homes. I began to have nightmares at the thought of the gruesome death of my sister. I dealt with hatred in my heart toward my brother-in-law, her husband. He had been abusive to her during their ten-year marriage. We just couldn't get her to leave him permanently. She certainly lived through the cycle of abuse! Thank God for my church family who prayed for me and supported me through these trying times.

The following year (1979) my youngest brother, Edward (Buck) was killed in an automobile accident at the age of 19. He was enlisted in the U.S. Army and stationed at Ft. Hood, Killeen, TX. Buck was the youngest of 12 children. I'll never forget the cries of my Mom while standing at his casket crying out "My Baby! My Baby!" and fainting out of exhaustion & devastation. Life hurts when you feel so helpless.

The following year (1980) my oldest brother (Roy) died of a massive heart attack at the age of 42. Mom was hospitalized in Lafayette, La. at the time and my sister Eva and I were at her bedside. How do we inform her that her oldest child had died when she was hospitalized for a bad heart condition? So, I informed her Dr. and asked him to be present when we deliver this dreadful news to my Mom. When we informed her, she remained calm. It was as though she already knew. She asked, "did he suffer?" I responded "No, he died in his sleep." She appeared somewhat relieved but saddened. She instructed us to do what we needed to do. We traveled to Beaumont, TX and funeralized him there.

Through it all, I managed to finally complete an Associate of Arts Degree at San Antonio Jr. College and enroll in the bachelor's program at Southwest TX State University, San Marcos, TX. However, in 1981, tragedy struck the family again! My Dad suffered a stroke and was hospitalized. Two weeks later he passed away. My family had certainly taken a hit! But God strengthened us and brought us through it all. I was in my last semester prior to graduation. I couldn't concentrate. I managed to complete the requirements for my bachelor's degree and opted to receive my diploma through the mail! It had been a long educational journey, yet I couldn't experience the joy amidst the tragedies! No more lectures from Dad, no more parables, no more words of wisdom, no more humor, no more of his dancing. Yet we were expected to move on. Nevertheless, his words live within us today. Well, Mom insisted on keeping my sister Ella's four children; she didn't want them separated.

Military Service

I learned from experience that no matter how many interruptions, downfalls or challenges we face in life, determination always pays off! Stay focused, stay with it, and you will accomplish what you set out to accomplish. Winners never quit, and quitters never win. In the midst of tragedies, I was promoted to a position working in the Intelligence Field at Kelly AFB. "Getting my foot in the door" was apparently working for me. By this time also, I knew how to depend on the Lord, in good times and bad. I knew how to "cast my anxiety on Him because He cares for me" (1 PE 5:7). In the midst of all tragedies, I learned to depend on Him to bring me and my family through, and He did just that. I am forever grateful of His Love, Mercy, and Faithfulness.

Determination does pay off; however, it can be costly. With full time employment, full time school, Reserve duty, a two-year-old daughter and twelve-year-old stepsons at home, I hadn't realized that stress had taken its toll! Yet adjusting to married life I may say, and feeling that hubby needed to be more engaged only compounded my stress! During my employment at Kelly AFB, I suffered two miscarriages within a 2-year period. Devastating as it was, I yet desired and yearned for more children. So, I began to condition my body, to eat healthily, to get serious about my spiritual life and to seek the Lord.

Three years later, at the age of 15, the boys returned to Charleston, SC to live with their mother. We missed them, and it was painful to watch the loneliness particularly experienced by Nat, now 5 years old. She continued to ask, "When is Michael and Daryl coming back?" It was hard on her, she missed them so. We assured her that we would visit them soon.

Well, my prayers were answered, and on December 17, 1980, we were blessed with our second beautiful and healthy baby girl, Chastity Yvette Gathers, weighing 7 lbs. 6 oz. A proud and happy Mother, I was! She resembled her Dad from day 1, and still does today! Chastity was born at Santa Rosa Hospital, San Antonio, TX.

I experienced complications immediately after delivery and underwent an emergency dilation and curettage (D&C) procedure. I'm still thankful today for my experienced Dr. who knew what to do. A week later I was released to bring my new baby home.

We had joined the local church, Joy Temple Church of God in Christ (COGIC). It was a spiritual elevation for me, as my years in New Mexico had been "rocky." Rocky job, rocky marriage, rocky assignment! Just rocky! There had been only one COGIC in Alamogordo, NM; The church had undergone a split due to factions within, and neither church was thriving. Consequently, I had lost momentum, joined up with some un-churched friends and went back to drinking and partying. It wasn't the best choice, I admit. However, at Joy Temple I regained my spiritual ground and began to thrive again spiritually. I met new friends who were very helpful to me, both in ministry and with the rearing of my children. This particular church had a large population of members in my age group (late 20's/early 30's). This was needful for me. I began to teach bible studies, I joined the church choir, and I became active in various auxiliaries. My Pastor recognized me as an "Aspiring Missionary," a title given to women called to Ministry, as the denomination did not ordain women as preachers then. I was licensed as a "Missionary" under his leadership. But the love of Christ and the love of His Word overshadowed denominational bylaws; it didn't matter that I was not ordained a preacher, elder or minister. I just welcomed the opportunity to teach and "expound" on God's word!

Well, a house divided will not stand (Mark 3:25). While I was active in the church and my husband chose not to be, this discord became so tough that I didn't want to continue in the marriage. We were driven apart for more reasons than one, and no longer functioned as a unit. After careful thought and consideration of the future for myself and now two children, I pondered re-entry into military service. I considered the security it would provide and its retirement benefits as well. I filed for a divorce due to

Military Service

incompatibility and irreconcilable differences, as I thought the marriage should be dissolved. After a year of separation, three years of working civil service and being an active reservist, I re-entered military service and focused on serving at least twelve additional years to retire with 20 years active military service. Also, I was really missing the military and traveling then.

Re-Entry into Military Service - 1981

I met with an Air Force Recruiter and sought to re-enter active military service. Unfortunately, I was told by the Air Force Recruiter that the Air Force had already met its "prior-service quota" for the year, and that I would have to wait until the next fiscal year to re-enter. I didn't want to wait; I wanted to get away. As I was leaving the Air Force Recruiter's Office, an Army Recruiter right next door motioned me to come into his office. I did. He gave me his Army pitch, looked at my record, and offered me a position in Environmental Science. He said "you won't have to repeat basic training, just enlist for three years. You'll train right here at Ft Sam Houston, and if you don't like it after three years, just get out." Well, that sounded good, but I wasn't ready for the Army. I inquired about the Officer Commissioning School (OCS), since I now held a bachelor's degree. Well, I was administered the qualification exam and was told I missed it by 5 points. Sadly, the entrance qualification was higher for females than for male applicants. Had I been a male applicant, my score would have qualified me! I thought, how unfair! I believe the rules have changed since then. I left the Recruiters office feeling so defeated! I returned and continued to work at Kelly AFB.

Circumstances in my personal life did not improve, rather, they grew worse. I reevaluated my personal life and my plans one day and returned to the Army Recruiter. Long story short, I reentered the military, U.S. Army, with plans to complete 12 additional years of active military service, which would qualify me for a 20-year retirement. So, I was stationed at Fort Sam Houston, and trained in Environmental Science, just as the Recruiter had promised. I enjoyed this new found job. It was very interesting to me. I appreciated once again a military environment.

In the Environmental Science training, I learned about air sampling, water sampling & purification, entomology, industrial hygiene, food service sanitation, health inspections, environmental inspections, communicable disease, and the like. I learned to inspect barber shops, beauty shops, food service establishments, hospitals, waste disposal systems, field hospitals, field water supplies, swimming pools and water sources. Upon completion of training, I was assigned to the Infection Control Unit at Brooke Army Medical Center, still at Ft. Sam Houston. My Boss, LtCol Ellen Gaynor, was such a great leader and mentor. She was concerned about the progression of her subordinates and pushed us to maximum potential, to do our best, just as my Dad had done.

**U.S. Army, Field Training Exercise
Ft. Sam Houston, TX (1982)**

Well, the divorce never happened. Things got better with counseling, and we were reconciled. On December 12, 1982, we were blessed with our third beautiful and healthy baby girl,

Military Service

LeKeisha Ellen Gathers. Col Gaynor accompanied my husband and me to the labor and delivery room. She was like a Lamaze coach. She stayed with me until I delivered and was moved to my room. When she left, my husband appreciated her so much that he replaced the middle name I had chosen (Annette) with Ellen, in appreciation of my Boss. LeKeisha, whose name I acquired from another baby's chart in the hospital, brought much joy to our lives, and still does today. Thank God for His bountiful blessings!

In 1983 I received orders to Landstuhl, Germany to serve a three-year tour. In order to accept the assignment, I had to reenlist. So, I did. Due to shortage of housing in the area, I had to travel alone to Germany while my husband and kids remained in Charleston, S.C. For the first time in his life, my husband was left in *full charge* of our three children! Yet he had help, as they stayed with his parents in Charleston, SC until the Army approved their travel. This was very convenient for the family, as the port they were to fly from was Charleston AFB.

Thank God for the friends I met at the Landstuhl Chapel in Germany. They assisted me in securing an apartment on the economy. I am forever grateful to the Jenkins family, Mack and Rosemary. They welcomed me into their home and provided the encouragement and support I needed. After work, they would take me to look for an apartment, which was scarce. After facing many disappointments, at the end of three months, I finally secured an apartment on the economy and my family was approved for travel. Brother Jenkins in his station wagon accompanied me to the airport to meet my family. Words cannot express how happy I was to see my family! My baby (Keisha) was only 15 months old, and she would not reach for me. This was painful, but I knew we'd overcome it. It didn't take long; I bribed her with lollipops and ice cream! I'm grateful to God for His bountiful blessings!

We were told prior to coming to Germany that "everyone who goes to Germany comes back with one of three things: a new car, a

German shrunk, or a baby." Well, I suppose we were greedy, because we came back with all three! An unexpected blessing occurred while stationed in Germany. We were blessed with our fourth beautiful daughter, Lauren Alaina Gathers. Surprised and unplanned as she may have been, she is truly a blessing from God! She was a blessing to the entire family; everyone spoiled her! My job was so supportive and showered her with blessings beyond measure. She lacked nothing. Again, I was blessed to have a wonderful sitter, which enabled me to continue my career without interruption.

My family loved Germany though it was freezing cold! However, it was beautifully white with snow. Germany has an excellent transportation system. We were able to travel a lot and visit many different countries. Germany is centrally located, so it wasn't uncommon to visit three countries in a day. We were 15 minutes from the French border. One could easily have breakfast in France, lunch in Belgium, dinner in the Netherlands and return home to Germany in the evening! We did that! The transportation system was impeccable! There was no speed limit on the autobahn (major highways). I'd say the average speed driven on the autobahn was 130 mph, and faster cars still passed you by. Our children loved it! They enjoyed making snowmen; they learned to ice ski. They even learned a few phrases in the German language while we lived on the economy for a year. Afterwards we were moved to Base housing.

Military Service

Zurich, Switzerland (1987)

In Germany we became affiliated with the Gospel Hr. Service, another turning point in my life! We met the most beautiful families and gained new friends, many of whom we are still in relationship with today. I became more deeply involved in ministry, preaching and teaching God's Word. After two years I enrolled in the Education Masters (Ed.M.) Degree Program with Boston University. Our church community was a very close-knit community. We visited each other regularly, even watched each other's kids. Had it not been for my church family and friends, taking night classes would have been difficult to impossible! My sister, Joyce, got stationed at Ramstein, Germany, less than 5 miles from us. What a Blessing! Then my first cousins, Larry and Ann joined us later. Our children grew up together in Germany. They loved playing together, making snowmen, throwing snowballs, and going volksmarching together. It was wonderful having family overseas! The children were able to have slumber parties in safe environments. They are still close-knit today!

In 1986 we faced another tragedy. While sitting at my desk one day, I was notified by the American Red Cross of the death of my Mom. She had had a massive heart attack in her sleep, just as my brother, Roy. I remember running to the bathroom at work, crying profusely! The German ladies were standing all around me trying to comfort me, but no words could comfort me. It just wasn't working. My Mom, our matriarch, our only parent, the wisdom of our family, our strength; how can we go on without her, I thought. But I had matured in the Lord, and somehow, I knew I'd be ok later on. One of my German friends drove me home, and I began to make preparations for our travel stateside to funeralize my Mom. Once again, my siblings and I rallied together and strengthened the bond one with another. This was *'déjà vu'* (already seen); we had been there before and knew what to do. I spoke at my Mom's funeral, which brought comfort to my siblings. My two older brothers (Lloyd and Floyd) were ever so proud and thanked me afterwards. In fact, my brother (Floyd) said, "when I die, I want you to do my funeral." What a request, I thought. Afterwards, we returned to Germany for the completion of my tour of duty.

Promotions continued for me. My family loved Germany so much that I extended twice. So, a 3-year tour was extended to 5 years. We continued to travel and enjoy the country. The church had annual retreats in Berchtesgaden, a beautiful city in southeastern Germany in the Bavarian Alps. Berchtesgaden borders Austria (where Adolf Hitler once had a fortified retreat) and is known for its alps, ski slopes, salt mine, majestic mountains, crystal clear lakes and its Alpine National Parks. Absolutely beautiful! We looked forward every year to going on retreats with the church, another highlight of our stay.

Salt Mine, Berchtesgaden, Germany (1987)

Military Service

"Sound of Music" filmed, Saltzburg, Austria

Again, hard work pays off! While in Germany, I completed all of the requirements for a Master's Degree in Education (Ed.M.) with Boston University. I also received a School-Guidance Counselor Certification from the State of Massachusetts.

Graduation, Boston Univ, Ed.M., (1988)

I completed the remainder of our five-year tour. It was now time for a career move. I applied for Instructor Duty at the Academy of Health Sciences, Fort Sam Houston, TX. and I was accepted! I reenlisted one last time and we prepared to leave Germany. It was hard leaving behind our family members, dear friends and church family that we loved so much.

Military Service

**U.S. Army Reenlistment
Landstuhl, Germany (1988)**

At the end of December 1988, we moved back to San Antonio, TX. The children missed Germany, their cousins and friends. They missed the snow. They would oftentimes ask "when are we going back to Germany?" and "when does it snow in San Antonio?" They missed making snowmen. Not in San Antonio! They oftentimes remarked, "I want to go back to Germany!" However, they were enrolled in the local schools and soon thereafter made new friends. Sometimes children adapt to change better than adults do!

Ethel Morale Gathers

I loved my job as an Instructor at the Academy. I taught students from all walks of life, including foreign, international students. I was blessed with wonderful bosses again. The training I had received 7 years prior all came into practice. As an Instructor, I was assigned various topics to teach, such as Industrial Hygiene, Food Service Sanitation, Cross Connections, Health Inspections, Water Purification, and Air Sampling. Instructor duty also entailed marching with the students to perform environmental and health inspections. Coupled with marching students was the physical training (PT) responsibilities, such as push-ups, sit-ups, jumping jack, and did I mention running? Because we trained with the students daily, as an Instructor my PT score was the best in my entire career! I was running 7 miles on my lunch hour, just because 😊. In fact, running in formation in the Army and singing cadence was fun, once I got in condition! Having served both branches of the military, I must admit, the Army's cadence was a bit more fun and upbeat than that of the Air Force!

> "C-130 rolling down the strip,
> Airborne ranger gonna take a little trip.
> Stand up, hook up, shuffle to the door,
> jump right out and count to four.
> If my main don't open wide,
> I got a reserve one by my side!
> A one, a two, a three, four hey!
> Run we gonna' run we gonna' run some more hey."

The lyrics were upbeat, in step, rhythmic; it kept the platoon together and in-step.

> "Up the hill, no sweat,
> down the hill, better yet.
> I can run to Georgia just like this,
> all the way to Ga I won't quit."

We'd run and sing cadence the entire hour! Torture it may have been at one time, however, when you got in condition it became

Military Service

fun! It was considered fitness, team building, camaraderie, all the good accolades! However, if you were not fit, it was torture! I was fit 😊.

At the same time that we were prospering naturally, we were also prospering spiritually. We were re-acquainted with former friends of ours at Wayfaring COGIC, where we had served for a year prior to moving to Germany. The pastor there, Pastor John Harvey, immediately recognized my call to Ministry. He appointed me as teacher over Young People Willing Workers (YPWW), an auxiliary focused on Bible study and increasing in the Word of God. I enjoyed teaching the Word of God then, and still do today. I love the enthusiasm of God's people when it comes to learning more about His Word and while discussing it to gain more insight. Practicing Bible drills was competitive and made learning fun.

A year later, my husband encountered a former friend who invited him to New Life Christian Center, an Interdenominational Church within five miles of our home. He visited the Church alone the first time. The kids and I were still attending Wayfaring COGIC. He returned home and told me about the Church and invited me to accompany him the following Sunday. So, we attended as a family. I loved the Church. The Pastor was a former military officer and was very orderly and precise in the operation of the Church. He was more of a teacher, as he had been a former Military Instructor. The praise and worship team were anointed. I remember the dance ministry; I loved to see them minister in dance. I knew then that I could easily join; but I loved the COGIC, I loved my Pastors and friends. So, when my husband approached me about joining New Life, I was torn. We had been ripped from our Landstuhl, Germany church family & friends a year prior, now he wants to rip us from our Wayfaring church family. So, he attended New Life a couple more Sundays and loved it. I spoke with my Pastor and shared my dilemma. After prolonged conversation he replied, "The chicken needs all eggs in the same basket," meaning the entire family needs to be together. He released me to join my husband, and we remain friends today. I continue to fellowship with them occasionally.

We joined New Life Christian Center on November 1, 1989, where God continued to prosper us as a family. To my surprise, I was re-acquainted with a few former friends who were members there. Our three younger children were enrolled at New Life Christian Academy, while Nat continued at John Jay High School. God prospered us academically, financially, naturally, and spiritually so. Praise God for His bountiful blessings!

At the end of five years, I retired from the US Army at the rank of Sergeant First Class. I'm very thankful of the times that I spent in the military: 8 years active-duty Air Force, 3 years AF Reserves, and 12 years active-duty U.S. Army. I'm grateful for the opportunity to have served my country. I'm very grateful for the opportunity that it afforded not only me, but my entire family, to travel abroad and to see the world. I'm grateful for the experiences—the good, the bad and the ugly! Above all, I'm grateful for the wonderful Christians that we met along the journey, some of whom we remain in contact today. I'm thankful for the pastors and leaders who mentored me spiritually. I'm grateful to God for having kept us these 23 years of military service. May God continue to bless this family. May God Bless America.

Military Service

Retirement from U.S. Army, May 1, 1993

CHAPTER 8

Post Military Service

Substitute Teacher

After military retirement I took a year break from the workforce. I had paid my dues and I felt that I deserved it! I enjoyed driving the children to school. Afterwards, I'd run about 10 laps around the church and school, totaling five miles. I was physically fit, having recently retired from the Army! I was able to focus more on the needs of my family. Don't ever think a "stay-at-home-Mom" has nothing to do! My Mom used to say, "A woman's job is never done." I found this to be true; A woman can always find "something" to do in the home! Just being able to cook breakfast in the morning without rushing, and having dinner prepared early in the evening was much appreciated by my husband and children!

After a year of being a homemaker, believe it or not, I started yearning for the workforce! I didn't want to be a stay-at-home Mom anymore. After all, I had a bachelor's degree in Business Management and a Master's in Education with a school guidance counselor certification. "For What?" I asked myself. One day I was sitting in church when one of the church members asked to see me after service. She was a Vice Principal at a local high school where my daughter, Nat, was attending. She informed me of the need for Substitute Teachers in the district and asked me was I interested.

Post Military Service

She said I would only work when I chose to; I could either "accept" or "decline" the request to work when called. Well, that interested me. So, I followed the necessary protocol and got registered as a Substitute Teacher. The very next day after I was accepted, I began to receive phone calls from various schools requesting a Substitute Teacher for the day. Any school in the district could call. I was being called DAILY! Wages were $50.00/day then (1993); Today it is $150/day. I began to accept jobs at the elementary schools, then the middle schools, then the high schools. EVERYDAY I'd get a request to teach! I guess I enjoyed it, because I never said no.

After doing this for approximately three months, I found myself going to work every day as a Substitute Teacher. While the pay was "ok" then, I knew I could qualify for jobs at a higher salary! So, I decided, if I'm going to work every day, let's make it worth my while; make the money commensurate with my credentials and abilities. I decided to update my resume and apply for jobs. I applied for a job with the County and got called the very next day! I interviewed for a position with The Center for Health Care Services (CHCS), the Mental Health/Mental Retardation (MHMR) Authority for Bexar County. This position required a master's degree. It was a rather strange interview, I thought, conducted by only one person. I expected a panel of some sort. After the interview, the Supervisor escorted me and introduced me to his boss who was also the Branch Chief. Then he escorted me throughout the organization, introducing me to other Supervisors. He then took me to his office and explained the position in its entirety. The position's title was "Continuity of Services Coordinator." He explained that the person in this position would work as a "Liaison" between the State Facilities and the Community, coordinating the mainstreaming individuals from State Facilities to group homes in the community and vice-versa. I had the nerve to tell him that I had "0" experience in working with the Mental Health/Mental Retardation population. He replied, "I read your resume, and if you did THIS in the military, you can do THAT here," as he pointed to the position description. He was a 65-

year-old German guy; his philosophy was quite different than that of many Americans! I must say, I liked his philosophy!

I returned home and told my husband how strangely the interview went. He replied, "Ethel, you got the job!" Well, nobody told me I had the job! However, the next day the call came, informing me of my selection for the position. I was scheduled to come in and complete the necessary paperwork. I must say I was nervous about going into a field which I had no experience in. But I remembered the voice of my Dad, "do your best," and, "that's not a hill for a stepper." I also recalled the scripture, "I can do all things through Christ who strengthens me." That was my motivator. I accepted the position as Continuity of Services Coordinator.

County Job

Working for the county was another brand-new career move. I learned a totally different culture and met different people from all walks of life. It was such a rewarding job, as I was able to help many families obtain resources in the community for their disabled loved ones. This position enabled me to travel throughout the State of Texas where State Facilities existed. After five years in the position, my supervisor, now 70, decided to retire. Well, another opportunity to excel! I interviewed for his position and was promoted to Management level. A few years later we re-organized (not by choice) and I was promoted to the position of Utilization Review Manager. This position called for the training and supervising of Case Managers, as well as the allocation of resources to families in need. Woah! New ballgame, but I could handle it, I told myself! The position became very stressful after re-organization. Regulations changed, state requirements increased, workloads increased, and there were high turn-over rates in case management. Yet we managed. I could still hear my Dad's teaching, *"travailler dur jamais tue personne"* (hard work never killed nobody) and his logic, *"sit tu travay dur, tu pap vole"* (if you work hard, you won't steal). That was his method of advising, short Creole phrases!

Post Military Service

After the adjustment period, I decided to further my education and use up my remaining educational benefits paid for by the federal government, called the GI Bill. I've always wanted to study Theology, so, I enrolled in the School of Theology at St. Mary's University. Two years later I obtained a Master of Arts degree in Theology. I found the field of theology very fascinating. I learned another way of "seeking the unsearchable riches of God!" After obtaining the degree, I began to teach Theology at our local church. The church had a School of Ministry, "New Life Living Word Seminary," which prepared students for ministry and ordination. Another rewarding position! Words cannot express the proud feeling of attending graduation ceremonies and witnessing the ordination of ministers whom I had a hand in instructing! They had met the requirements for ordination and were now becoming licensed Ministers.

New Life Christian Center was a progressive church; always on the move. Within approximately a five-eight-year period, the congregation teamed together, under the Leadership of our Pastors, and had a brand-new church, school, and nursery built. We soon thereafter expanded to the purchasing of a ranch, and had two homes, an administrative building and a B&B built on the grounds. These homes were to accommodate children from the system, Department of Family and Protective Services, who had fallen through the cracks of abuse, abandonment and neglect. I was blessed to spearhead the committee, whose tireless efforts and long hours of dedication, resulted in the church's certification and licensure to operate a General Residential Organization (GRO) in the State of Texas. This affords the children a place of love, hope, and restoration. The Bible states, *"Religion that God our Father accepts as pure and faultless is this: to look after orphans and widows in their distress and to keep oneself from being polluted by the world"* (James 1:17). Well, the Ranch did just that for the children in care, and still does today. May God bless the staff who continuously devote themselves to the wellbeing of the children in its care, the prosperity of the children who pass through, and the pastors who pursued this God-given vision.

Did I mention the travels sponsored by the church? Many who had never traveled abroad began to travel with the church. My family and I continued our travels, visiting such places as the Bahamas, Israel, Greece, and Africa:

Jerusalem, Israel (November 1996)

Post Military Service

Western Wall, Jerusalem, Israel (November 2000)

Garden Tomb, Israel (November 2000)/

Dead Sea, Israel (November 2000)

Post Military Service

Israel (November 2000)

Olympic Stadium: Athens, Greece

Ethel Morale Gathers

After 15 years with the Center for Health Care Services and loving the autonomy which the job afforded me, our department was merged with another organization. This merge did not go well for us, to say the least! This particular organization practiced micro-management and did not permit leaders to lead, as we were accustomed. It was totally different from the former organization. Morale decreased, case managers began to leave the organization, we experienced high turnover rates. It was not good. At the same time, my husband was suffering from complications of diabetes and other ailments. He had scheduled medical appointments at least twice a week. Our children had grown up and were either in college or living independently. I was his only help, and the organization was not as supportive as the first. After two years, I resigned my position with the new organization and chose to be at home with my husband. I accompanied him to all of his medical appointments. On a good day (health wise), we would take drives along the country roads to Prairie View A&M University where our youngest daughter, Alaina, was attending. We would stop at flea markets, farmers markets and thrift stores along the way, enjoying the beauty of the little country towns. Of course, his health improved 😊. I'm thankful for those days! I believe that's when I slowly started retiring from the kitchen! He liked to eat out, and I surely didn't mind! It was only the two of us and that was fine.

After two years at home with my husband, another opportunity presented itself! Sitting in the church again, a friend of mine approached me after service and asked, "do you want a job?" I replied, "I'm not looking, but what do you have in mind?" She held a high position within the federal government. She explained the expansion of the organization she worked in and her need to hire more people. This position almost doubled the salary of my previous position, the one from which I had resigned. It was a Program Analyst position with the United States Air Force. I returned home from church and shared the information with my husband. Without hesitation he said, "take it!" I asked who was going to accompany him to his hospital appointments and who was

Post Military Service

going to monitor his sugar levels, etc. He replied, "Ethel, you've tried to enter civil service before, and the window of opportunity was closed. Do you think perhaps this is a blessing from God?" Well now, it's amazing how we ask God for something and when we don't get it right away, we soon forget our petition. After pondering for a few weeks, I told my friend "Let's go for it." At the opportune time, interviews were held, and I was selected to return to civil service at Lackland AFB as a Program Analyst. Praise God from whom all blessings flow!

CHAPTER 9

Federal Civil Service & Retirement

I began a new career, this time with the federal government at Lackland Air Force Base. How interesting! I was returning to the Air Force where I began my initial career as a Basic Trainee at the age of 18. Returning to Lackland after thirty-seven years was somewhat like the twilight zone! Everything looked so different. We were now in the Cyber-age and much of the terminology had changed. The mission had expanded. I had to learn the Air Force all over again. New Commands had been established to keep up with the changing times. It was all new but a rewarding experience. I learned the new job quickly and made new friends.

I enjoyed working with the military once again. The conversations were totally different with my new co-workers than they had been while working the social system with the county. I began learning the way of the military all over again, not that I had totally forgotten, but much was new. Participating in commander's call and attending promotion and retirement ceremonies helped with the process. I recall being asked to pray over a meal at a special event. It wasn't long before I would be asked to pray at all special events: retirement ceremonies, promotion ceremonies, change of command ceremonies, Air Force birthdays, and holiday events. It was an honor to be asked.

I learned my job as a Program Analyst, working in such jobs as Risk Management, Compliance Officer performing inspections of the organization, and finally Support Agreements Manager, developing and managing Agreements and Contracts for the Air Force. I excelled at my job. I was selected to be the "Resiliency Trainer" for my Branch, conducting whatever didactic training the Air Force or higher headquarters deemed necessary for its airmen, civilians included. I enjoyed being a Trainer; seems that I could never escape "the calling" of an Instructor/Teacher/Trainer. I reflected on my high school days when my teacher had asked what was my goal after high school. I replied, "to go to college and become a teacher." She suggested I was aiming too high, that I should consider becoming a librarian or secretary instead. Looking back, I now realize that God knew all along what I was destined to be, a teacher. I realize also that my *entire adult life* has been that of a teacher, in one capacity or another: Sunday school teacher, instructor duty with the military, training case managers, Resiliency trainer for the Air Force, instructor at the theological seminary, substitute teacher in public schools, teaching at conferences and seminars, leading workshops, heading ministries. Yes, my entire life has been that of a teacher!

I enjoyed "down days" when the organization participated in team-building exercises. We were so competitive, even in games! We would team-up according to Branch we worked in and walk two miles together as an organization. Afterwards, we would compete against each other in such sports as basketball, volleyball, and track & field events. This promoted physical fitness as well as organizational unity and offered a relaxing day away from work!

While excelling at my job, I was also growing spiritually. My Pastor's had accepted an opportunity to bring TORAH Studies to the church, taught by Jewish Rabbis. Of course, I enrolled! The purpose of the course was to introduce (and return) us to the "Hebraic Roots of Our Faith." The course was divided into a five-part series, taught over the course of five years. The class met once a week. As in regular school, we were administered exams. At the end of each series, we participated in a small graduation ceremony and were awarded a course completion certificate from the Simchat TORAH Beit Midrash (Joy of the Torah, House of Study), Denver, CO. The eyes of my understanding were certainly enlightened by the study of the TORAH, to the Hebraic roots of our faith. Words cannot express the spiritual growth and insight gained from this study. Today, I teach some of the lessons to different audiences. Suffice to say, I was one of the honor graduates of the last series! What a Blessing!

The congregation was increasing in knowledge of the Word. Those who wanted to grow in the Lord certainly had the opportunity; there was no shortage of the Word. A few years later, we were offered another opportunity to engage in a different study—reading the Bible through-and-through within a year. The only book used was *"The Daily Bible" New International Version (NIV), Copyright © 1984 by Harvest House Publishers, Eugene, Oregon.* This particular Bible lists *"In Chronological Order, 365 Daily Readings with Devotional Insights to Guide You Through God's Word."* I cite this reference because I highly recommend it for your library, but mostly for learning purpose and spiritual growth. It is an "easy read" and guarantees the reading of the entire Bible, all 66 books, within a year if you follow the daily readings.

Again, the course was conducted in a relatively competitive manner. We were placed in groups of threes, which made the course fun and promoted new friendships within the assigned groups. We tested together by group. After the test, we would exchange papers, score them, and occasionally compare scores. Based on these comparisons, it was known that my group was in the lead; we had scored 100 on ALL of the exams throughout the year! Well, a *strange thing* happened on the day of graduation. After being presented our certificates of completion, the two Valedictorians were announced and brought on stage before the entire congregation. Much to my chagrin, it was NOT me or any of the two in my group! I was shocked, my children were shocked, my group was shocked, my Team Leaders were shocked, even the two people being recognized were shocked! How can this be? So, I sat through the service after the ceremony, partially dissociated! I couldn't shake it mentally. So, immediately after the service I met with one of my Team Leads who said she would look into it; she was shocked as well. Let's just conclude that I was not invited to the review or discussion. I was not allowed to compare the scores of the so-named valedictorians with the scores of my group, and the decision stood firm. Therefore, the term, *"It is what it is"* became real to me! This tactic was not new. *déjà vu!* I had seen it before! I just didn't expect to see it in the church! I quickly embraced the fact that God is bigger than that! Again, I recalled the teaching of my parents, "what God has given you, no man can take away," and I moved on from this disappointment also.

While I continued to excel at my job and life was good, tragedy struck my family in 2012 when my husband became solemnly ill. Diabetes had taken its toll on his kidneys and the hospitalizations began again. After three days of him being hospitalized, I remember telling my boss one day that I was going to Bill Millers BBQ and get some beef soup w/rice for my husband, one of his favorites. I told her that I was going to the hospital and have him discharged and brought home. Well, I arrived at the hospital only to find him in a diabetic coma! I was so shocked, mad, hurt, annoyed, disappointed, bewildered, you name it. No one from the hospital had notified me. I had a few choice words for the doctors and staff (not cuss words). From that day I remained in the hospital at my husband's side. After a few overnights in his hospital room, a few of my friends, sisters and daughters began to relieve me. They would tell me to go home and rest, while they remain at my husband's bedside, because I didn't want him left alone. I'd try to rest at home, but it was hard staying away. I'd be back at the Hospital the next morning. I would talk to him and read the Bible to him even though he could not respond. This caught the attention of a few of the hospital staff and they began to ask me questions about the Bible and "what church do you go to?" God afforded me an opportunity to witness (and to teach), and I took it. I had a "tallit" (Jewish prayer shawl) on my husband's bed. One day a nurse asked me the meaning of the prayer shawl. Well, this began a study of the tallit, right there in the Intensive Care Unit of the hospital! Every day she would stop by to learn more about the tallit. This went on for two weeks. Thank God for the opportunity to teach those who are eager to learn!

Well, my husband never recovered from the diabetic coma. In fact, he developed pneumonia during this 2-week hospital stay. On February 8, 2012, my husband passed away. My pastor would sometimes say, "you never realize that God is all you need until God is all you have." Suddenly, I knew what it meant. I felt so weak, alone, and lost, even with my family by my side. Yet I knew my children and grandchildren were drawing their strength from me. So, I prayed to the Lord for strength, and the Lord provided. He is a very present help in times of trouble. Daryl and Michael, his sons, flew in from Columbus, Ga. What a reunion it was with our 4 daughters. Through his death, my husband had managed to bring his six children together, it had been a while! It brought joy to my heart to hear the laughter, the storytelling, and to witness the sweet commune of the six.

Children: Daryl, Michael, Nathasha, Chastity, LeKeisha, Alaina

My husband was funeralized at our local Church. With the strength of God, I did the eulogy. All of my co-workers attended. My siblings were there, as always, as were my in-laws from TN. My Pastors and church family were also present and a great source of strength to me. Church members showered my family with love, meals, transportation, and just overall support! My organization did likewise. I'll never forget the postcard I received in the mail one day. It was from my Company Commander, hand-written, expressing his condolences and advising me, "Don't worry about the job; come back only when you are ready." What a blessing that was! So, I remained home for a month. My two younger brothers (Black & Ken) stayed with me that month, though they lived in Arizona! Oh, what love the Father has bestowed upon me through my siblings; I am forever grateful! Upon return to work, my Boss and my co-workers welcomed me back and continued to provide the mental support that I needed.

In November of 2019, we suffered another loss among siblings. My brother (Floyd) from Beaumont, TX had been ill for quite some time and had been living in a Nursing Facility. My siblings and I would rally around him as often as we could. Sometimes all you can give a person is Love, but remember, it is the greatest gift! Floyd knew his days were numbered, so are ours. I can recall the last time I visited him, he called us to his bedside one-by-one and kissed our hand. He could no longer speak, yet he recognized us to the end. I knew he was saying goodbye to us. 1 Thessalonians 5:18 tells us to *"give thanks in all circumstances, for this is God's will for you in Christ Jesus."* So, I gave thanks to God for allowing my brother to live 78 years. I thank Him for allowing my brother to communicate with us, and to recognize us to the end. I thank God that his spirit man was prepared and ready to meet the Lord. He passed away peacefully.

Well, weeping may endure for a night, but joy comes in the morning. As a family, we managed to pull ourselves up from our bootstraps (Army saying) and grab a hold of life again! A few of us decided on a trip to Australia and New Zealand. Why not? So, in December 2019, I joined a group of six family members and retired Air Force friends and headed for Australia and New Zealand. It was so refreshing; we had a wonderful time, much needed! Two years prior, the same group of seven had traveled to Egypt, toured the pyramids and other exclusive sights in Egypt. Thank God for these wonderful opportunities and His traveling mercies.

Federal Civil Service & Retirement

Cairo, Egypt (July 2017)

Cairo, Egypt (July 2017)

Wellington, New Zealand (December 2019)

At Sea, New Zealand (December, 2019)

**Bonorong Wildlife Sanctuary
Tasmania, Australia (December 2019)**

Retirement

I worked ten additional years at LAFB, then one day I started contemplating retirement. I'd tell my co-workers, "I'm thinking about retiring." They'd respond, "you're not going anywhere." This went on for three years. In the thirteenth year, I announced again that I'm contemplating retirement. Of course, they didn't believe me; I had "cried wolf" three years in a row! However, I completed my retirement application packet in early January 2020 and requested a retirement date of 29 February 2020. My Boss and co-workers were surprised. "She's really going through with it this time," they said. Yes, I went through with it! My Branch gave me a nice retirement luncheon and showered me with gifts and accolades. My children, siblings and some of my friends from the church were present. I was presented several awards, so were my children. It was a beautiful day with wonderful fellowship. I'm so grateful to my God for sustaining me these years in the workforce. He is faithful to His promises and to those who call upon His Name. On February 29, 2020, I officially retired from federal civil service, totaling 50 years in the workforce. I'm grateful to God for all of my assignments and experiences!

Retirement from Civil Service

Federal Civil Service & Retirement

Retirement luncheon

All of my careers were wonderfully successful! I'm very thankful to have had the traveling opportunities that I dreamed of as a little girl. I am very thankful to have had the best of military service, to include medical and dental privileges for myself and my family. I'm grateful for the various schools my children attended and the teachers who poured into their lives. I'm grateful for the travel opportunities it afforded my family. I'm grateful for the various pastors during my career, and the mentorship they provided. I'm especially grateful for the pastors and Leaders who groomed me in ministry and trusted me in the delivery and teaching of God's Word, my delight! My work history was just an overall blessing, and I am forever grateful.

CHAPTER 10

Post Retirement (Present)

After retirement from civil service my plan was to travel. I had prayed and asked God to allow me to visit all seven continents, well, excluding Antarctica, before leaving this earth. As of now, God has blessed me to visit all, with the exception of South America. So, I had planned to visit Brazil upon retirement. I also made plans to visit three of my ex-military friends in Georgia, Colorado and New York.

So, immediately upon retirement I began my travels by accompanying my sister, Joyce, to Las Vegas. Her son, Jason, was starring in a play that he had written, *"PATII"*. My brother, Black, met us there. The play was so wonderfully amusing, as well as educational; we saw it twice! We had a great time. I left Vegas and traveled with my brother to San Tan Valley, AZ, just outside Phoenix. I had planned on staying a week with him, then visit my friend, Georgia, in Denver Co. first, Gloria in New York second, and Pastor Deborah in Savanah, Georgia, third. However, while in AZ we were notified that my oldest brother (Lloyd) age 80, in Kansas City, MO. was very ill. He required emergency surgery and prognosis was poor. So, I decided to leave AZ and travel to MO. instead, to be with him. While in MO., we entered into a pandemic in March 2020 which changed the whole world. The entire Country

Post Retirement (Present)

went into lockdown due to the coronavirus and I was told that if I left the Hospital, I would not be able to reenter, so I stayed. The Hospital was very "hospitable" to me, gave me free room and board, allowed me to room with my brother and to care for him. My sister (Mercedes) was there with me for one week, then she returned home to Longview, TX.

The first week while I was there, my brother was conscious and verbal. I was the liaison between him and the rest of the family. He was able to speak to the family, and vice-versa, joking as his custom was. I would send pictures of him to the family; they would also face-time him. My brother and I had many heart-to-heart conversations. As days progressed, he was also able to say his goodbyes to the family in MO. I watched my brother slowly fade away, ministering to him daily and reading the Bible to him, which he enjoyed. Watching the process of death unfold right before my eyes was hard and draining. However, during these times, I drew strength from the Lord. My brother loved the Lord and had lots of moments of reconciliation. He was a jokester and found humor in everything; a coping mechanism I believe. He felt that his end was near. He loved for me to pray with him. I suspected a lot of reconciliation was taking place.

During this hospital stay, I petitioned the Lord about many "cares." The Bible says, *"cast all your cares upon Him because He cares for you"* (1 Pe 5:7), so I did. This time of solemnity was greatly needed for me! While my brother slept, I prayed, questioning the Lord on many things. I inclined my ears to hear and sought His guidance for my own life. I was in mental turmoil, sadly but particularly over things pertaining to the ministry. I just wanted to be in the center of His will, doing what He called and anointed me to do, which was to teach and preach His Word and to win souls. I questioned whether I was yet called to the church I had been a member of for thirty years! I was so uneasy about not freely flowing in ministry, as called. A paradigm shift had occurred in the ministry, particularly affecting the use of elders and ministers. It was on a decline, for whatever reason. Besides, God had given me a Work, the Ministry of "Dedicated Women in Christ (DWIC)," president of the San Antonio Chapter, which was now successfully in its third year of operation and growing.

I was seeking the Lord on "how" I was to flow in that work since it appeared to have become a source of conflict with my own church. The church that I loved and had been a part of for thirty years had gradually become an inward struggle for me. Attending services three times a week, with the same "uneasy" feelings persisted. I later learned that there was *speculation* that I would start my own church and thereby "split" the church! (Vexation of spirit saith the preacher!) How was I to continue this work in the midst of such opposition? I had requested an appointment with Leadership (twice), wanting to clear the air and put to death any false rumors. However, the turning point was when I was not granted access on the two occasions I sought. This *really* threw me into perplexity! After all, I was a "Ruling Elder," along with two other Ruling Elders, second position in the leadership chain, yet I was denied an appointment? Wow! On this, I seriously sought the Lord for guidance, daily.

After three weeks of sharing a room with my brother in the Hospital, he passed away peacefully. I'm grateful for the time which God allowed me to spend with him. I remained in K.C. an extra couple of days, shadowing my sister-in-law as she finalized funeral arrangements. When everything was settled, I departed K.C., MO. and returned home to San Antonio. The plane ride was rather dreary! I couldn't sleep on the plane, so I just read and looked out the window at the clouds. I was thankful of the COVID-19 standards being adhered to. I had a row of seats to myself for the first time in my life! I was drained - physically, mentally and spiritually. Suddenly I was reminded of the saying of Peter and the other Apostles, "we must obey God rather than man" (Acts 5:29). I pondered those words for a while; I couldn't shake them.

Post Retirement (Present)

I returned home to San Antonio, the country still on lockdown. Daily I continued to bask in the memories of my brother and the time I spent with him. I continued meditating on my prayers and petitions before the Lord. I pondered the words again, "we must obey God rather than man." Suddenly, I felt that my prayers were answered! I knew the way forward for my life! I knew I had to pursue the ministry the Lord had given me, "Dedicated Women in Christ (DWIC)." I knew that I was to teach and preach His Word without apology! This was the "platform" He had given me to do so. Somehow, I knew also, that I was not returning to the Ruling Eldership position in my local church. When this divine inspiration came, I immediately called my friend, another Ruling Elder, and informed him that I would not be returning to the Eldership.

When churches were allowed to open again during the pandemic, I returned to my local church on a Sunday morning. It was an awkward feeling, as though I was a "visitor." I had been away for approximately six weeks. I sat in the balcony, totally unusual, as I was accustomed to sitting on the front row. But I was perfectly comfortable, because I *knew* I was not returning to the Eldership. I did this two other times, came to church on Sunday morning and sat in the balcony. After the third attendance, I was convinced in my spirit that I was to pursue greater works and obey the voice of Him who called me into Ministry. That day, I departed from a church I had served 30 years, to pursue the calling of God on my life.

I pray for the leadership of my church, that they would hear and obey the voice of the Lord. I wish well to all members, that the Lord prosper them in every way. I am thankful and grateful to the Pastors who introduced me to the Hebraic roots of our faith, and who poured into me these past 30 years. Now, I must obey God rather than man, and work the works of Him who sent me while it is day. My gift and calling from the Lord is to teach and to preach His Word. This I know, beyond the shadow of a doubt. I am passionate for His Word, with the passion which He has placed inside me. I continue to serve my Lord and Savior, Jesus Christ. I walk by faith, not by sight, and I live in the hope of His return. All that I have accomplished, I owe it all to Him. My breath, my desires, my ability comes from Him.

Like the prodigal son, I *"came to myself"* and suddenly became focused! I knew I was to continue with the Women's Ministry. In retirement I also knew that it was time to focus on unfinished goals. I had several unfinished projects, such as completing the Doctoral Degree Program which I had begun years prior, AND, writing books. I was mopping my floors one day, and suddenly I could not shake off the words "CHURCH CULTURE." After hearing it three times, I came to my kitchen table and began to write *"CHURCH CULTURE: What Members Dare Not Say."* Within the next few minutes, I had written down the titles of 10 Chapters. I believe this to have been divinely inspired by the Holy Spirit; therefore, I began to write. Day after day, the chapters unfolded. Morning till evening, I wrote intermittently. When I couldn't sleep, I would get up and write. One day my daughter (Nat) said to me, "Mom when you finish this book your next book needs to be about yourself!" This idea was also echoed by my youngest daughter, Alaina. I jokingly responded, "I know all about myself, I don't need to write about myself." Nat replied, "it's not for you Mom, it's for us, and generations after us!"

So, in September 2020, my first book was published: *"CHURCH CULTURE: What Members Dare Not Say."* (Available on Amazon, Barnes & Nobel, and at ethelgathers.carrd.co).

Post Retirement (Present)

"CHURCH CULTURE: *What Members Dare Not Say*"

The book was very successful and soon thereafter became a useful Bible Study tool in several churches. It is currently being reviewed for use as a textbook by a few Bible Colleges. God is so good and faithful!

In the midst of celebrating my newly published book, we faced another tragedy five months after the passing of my brother, Lloyd. We were notified of the passing of my sister in Longview (Mercedes), who had been with me in K.C., MO caring for our brother. This was a shock to the entire family! She was 72 years of age. We were together five months prior! Little did I know that it would be the last time I would be with her on this earth. So, off we went to Longview, TX and did what we knew to do. I find that one thing about death is, it is certain, it is final, it is unpredictable. I am thankful to have spent a week with her, a good week of laughter, prayer, and sharing of God's Word. I find also that God's promises are "Yes and Amen!" So, we continue to live and await the coming of our Lord and Savior, Jesus Christ, and the life He has prepared for us in the world to come. Therefore, I am comforted by His Word.

While continuing down the education lane, I was also able to complete all requirements for a Doctoral Degree in Religious Education. My sister, Joyce, also completed the requirements for a Doctoral in Guidance Counseling. The 2020 graduation ceremony was postponed due to COVID19. Therefore, the 2020 graduates were permitted to participate in the 2021 commencement ceremony. What a joy it was to graduate together! Inwardly I sensed the approval and pridefulness of our parents; I only wished they could have been present. However, God has a way of taking our mourning and turning it into dancing! He takes away our grief and turns it into joy!

Post Retirement (Present)

**Doctoral Graduation
September 30, 2020**

**Doctoral Graduation
July 10, 2021**

Post Retirement (Present)

The Scripture, *"I can do all things through Christ who strengthens me"* (PH 4:13) became alive in me again, as I saw the Holy Spirit directing my path, and feeling great about it! I had been released in my spirit to pursue with passion the gift and calling of God on my life, and Life was Good! When we are weak, He is made strong.

I now serve alongside pastors of the local Faith-Based Institute Church, whose proud logo is, "A Church in the Streets." This Ministry is committed to doing the works which Christ commissioned, to save souls, to feed the hungry, to clothe the naked, to shelter the homeless, to see about the widows and orphans. This church recognized and accepted the calling of God on my life and allows me to flow freely in the ministry of teaching and preaching. This church also welcomes and supports the Ministry of Dedicated Women in Christ (DWIC). This is what I had been praying for, to be used in God's service. God has brought new friends into my life. It is liberating to serve the Lord. Oh, how good and pleasant it is for brothers to dwell together in unity (Psalm 133:1).

I praise God for the years of life He has granted me on earth. On November 15, 2021, I celebrated my 70th birthday, sponsored by my current church, Faith-Based Institute – A Church in the Streets. Oh, what a joy it was, to be celebrated by friends and family. My entire "clan of 20" were present: children, grand-children and great grandchildren.

Ethel Morale Gathers

70th Birthday Party, November 15, 2021

Post Retirement (Present)

**70th Birthday Party: My Clan of 20
Children, Grandchildren, Great-grandchildren**

**70th Birthday Party
Grandsons, Sons-in-Law/Love**

Post Retirement (Present)

Friends from my former church came to celebrate me; this was so special to me. The fun and laughter, the celebration, words cannot express! I am forever grateful!

To my children, my children's children, my great-grandchildren, and all generations to come: May you know Christ in the pardon of your sins, receive Him as Lord and Savior according to Romans 9:10, know Him in the power of His resurrection according to Philippians 3:10, and walk in the light of God's Word. May you seek the gift of the Holy Spirit according to Acts, Chapter 2. He has set before you life and death, choose life so that you and your children may live (Deut. 30:19). Words cannot express my perpetual Love for you!

My Autobiography.

Ethel Morale Gathers (Aka Mom, Grand-Ma, Honey-Child, Honey, Lou, Elder Gathers, Dr. Gathers).

NOTES

From Wikipedia, the free encyclopedia

1. The **Treaty of Fontainebleau** was a secret agreement of 1762 in which the Kingdom of France ceded Louisiana to Spain. The Treaty was kept secret even during the French negotiation and signing of the Treaty of Paris (1763), which ended the war with Great Britain and divided Louisiana at the Mississippi. The eastern half was ceded to Great Britain, and the western half and New Orleans were nominally retained by France.

2. The **Cajuns** (/ˈkeɪdʒən/; Louisiana French: *les Cadiens*), also known as *Acadians* (Louisiana French: *les Acadiens*),[3] are an ethnic group mainly living in the states of Louisiana and Texas, and in the Canadian Maritimes provinces consisting in part of the descendants of the original Acadian exiles—French-speakers from Acadia (*L'Acadie*) in what are now the Maritimes of Eastern Canada.

3. The term **Créole** was originally used by French settlers to distinguish persons born in Louisiana from those born in the mother country or elsewhere. As in many other colonial societies around the world, creole was a term used to mean those who were "native-born," especially native-born Europeans such as the French and Spanish. It also came to be applied to African-descended slaves and Native Americans who were born in Louisiana. The word is not a racial label, and people of fully European descent, fully African descent, or of any mixture therein including Native American admixture may identify as Creoles.

4. **Louisiana Creole people** (French: *Créoles de la Louisiane*, Spanish: *Criollos de Luisiana*) are persons descended from

the inhabitants of colonial Louisiana during the period of both French and Spanish rule. Louisiana Creoles share cultural ties such as the traditional use of the French, Spanish, and Louisiana Creole languages and predominant practice of Catholicism. The region became a major center of both Cajun culture and Creole culture in Louisiana. European Americans and African Americans both adhered to the French-influenced culture and language, as well as absorbing and sharing aspects of African American and Native American cultures, including food.

REFERENCES

1. Chidsey, Donald Barr. *Louisiana Purchase*. Crown Publishers, Inc., New York. 1972.

2. Kubler-Ross, Elisabeth. *On Death and Dying.* New York: The Macmillan Company. 1969.

3. Lee, Robert. *"The True Cost of the Louisiana Purchase."* Slate. Retrieved October 1, 2019. http://www.slate.com/articles/news_and_politics/history/2017/03/how_much_did_the_louisiana_purchase_actually_cost.html

4. Managan, Kathe. *The Term "Creole" in Louisiana: An Introduction Archived*. The Wayback Machine, San Francisco, CA. December 5, 2013 lameca.org.

5. The Gordon Parks Foundation. "Segregation in the South," 1956 Photography Archive. gordonparksfoundation.org

6. United States Census Bureau. From Wikipedia, the free encyclopedia.

Additional Family Pictures

Aunt Clara Morale, age 102, Family Matriarch (July 2021)

Morale Family (1978)

Siblings & Me (1993)

Additional Family Pictures

**At Floyd's passing
October 5, 2019**

Husband, Richard A. Gathers & Me
(July 26, 1945 - February 8, 2012 - RIP)
(Nov 15, 2011)

Additional Family Pictures

Morale Family Reunion, September 2021

Ethel Morale Gathers

70th birthday party; dancing with Grandkids

COLLAGE

Ethel Morale Gathers

Collage

About the Ministry

DEDICATED WOMEN IN CHRIST (DWIC) MINISTRY

San Antonio, Texas Chapter

Ethel Gathers, President

Cell: (210) 618-7107; egathers@att.net; www.dwic1.com
Mary Wooldridge, Vice President
(210) 445-9539; marywooldridge@att.net

About the Ministry

A Ministry given in prayer, to a small group of women in Landstuhl, Germany, 1986.

DWIC expanded to Four Chapters in the United States with Headquarters in Las Vegas, NV, and subsequent Chapters in Pensacola, FL., Batesville, MS. and San Antonio, TX.

Mission Statement: Women dedicated to loving, encouraging, and building each other in Christ by caring, sharing, and reaching out to others in Love. Tools of the Ministry include: Workshops, Seminars, Conferences, Retreats and Outreach.

** Dr. Ethel Gathers is an author and sought-after Speaker who ministers to all age groups

"CHURCH CULTURE: What Members Dare Not Say"

Available @ www.ethelgathers.carrd.co
Amazon, Barnes & Noble

www.ingramcontent.com/pod-product-compliance
Lightning Source LLC
Chambersburg PA
CBHW040318170426
43197CB00021B/2951